THE RED WING CHRONICLES

(A STREAM OF CONSCIOUSNESS PERSONAL EXORCISM)

BY

RON TERRANOVA

REaDLIPS Press

Managing Editors: Della Rey & Jack Odman.

Editor: Noreen Lace

Cover Art: Linda Joseph-Turek
Silver Moon Photography

THIS BOOK IS DEDICATED TO THE
SICK, SUFFERING AND ABUSED CHILDREN OF THE
WORLD. BE STRONG. PERSEVERE.

PREVAIL.

Editor's Note:
Portions of this book are written as stream of consciousness, a technique in which rules of traditional punctuation are suspended to affect a free flowing narrative not unlike a sustained jazz improvisation. What may appear to be run on sentences with sudden thematic shifts are by design.

Once again, it's 9:00 P.M. and I'm supine on the couch, my feet propped up on the couch's back, and I'm staring at my shoes. What are they called? Ah, yes, Red Wings. As if I didn't know.

They've seen some miles. Why are they called Red Wings, anyway? They're neither red, nor do they have wings. Red Wings. Sounds like crimson footwear worn by Hermes. Or is it Mercury? Same God, the former created by the Greeks, the latter a co-opted version of the Romans. Or so I seem to remember.

Staring at my shoes. I've grown so indolent, I don't seem to have the will to remove them. Indolence? Too harsh perhaps. More of a malaise- a lethargy of the body; a paralysis of the spirit. I suppose I could remove them, but to what purpose? I'd only have to put them on again at some point- I suppose.

How long have I been l laying here, staring at my shoes? They look scuffed. I have another pair I've barely worn. They're practically new. Only one way to keep them that way.

It's beginning to feel like I've always been lying on this couch, staring at my shoes. What if I have always been staring at them? Before I was born- before the beginning of time? What if before The Big Bang I was floating around in the void, on this couch, staring at these shoes? I suppose it would be hard to prove- or disprove, for that matter.

Maybe I should do something, make myself useful. But then again, how many wars, purges and holocausts were started by men who felt a need to be useful? It's a conundrum. More than a conundrum. A conundrum, wrapped in enigma, shrouded in paradox. Maybe I could do something positive, but one false move and I've flipped the lid off Pandora's Box. Pandora. Another character from Greek myth. I wonder if she knew Hermes? Would they be a fun couple? Hermes was fast. Maybe he could catch all those ills and evils and return them to Pandora's Box.

I saw something. I'm sure I did. The Red Wing shoe on my right foot, propped up on the back rest of the couch. It moved. Or, more likely, the foot inside the shoe moved. How odd. It must have been an involuntary muscular response- a tic of sorts. I didn't will my foot to move. I'm not responsible, so let's not do the blame game. Lethargy- immobility of the will- of the spirit has its virtues. If something bad happens- really bad- You can bet I didn't do it.

I wonder- just wonder, if the scuffing on my shoes can be buffed and polished away? I'd have to take them to the shoe shop. But that would necessitate getting up. I wonder if I could pull that off? Getting up, I mean. Ah well, I guess I'll never know.

Sometimes I remember things. Or at least I think I remember. What if we make memories up? What if we remember events that never happened? Or for that matter have forgotten events that did? But if they did happen, then our memories would be of other memories remembered over and over again, a little bit different each time. One of the bad memories: there's a girl. She's about nine. She's in a kitchen, cleaning something with a wire brush. It's an oblong box with holes in it. It's a washing machine filter, or so I remember. The girl is shoving the brush through the holes. I watch her, shoving the brush through the different holes. The memory. I remember being five. The girl is my sister.

I feel mischievous. I peek through some of the holes in the filter. Peek-a-boo. Then she shoves the brush and I scream. Two people whisk me away. They are my parents.

A doctor gently lifts my eyelid and looks into my eye with a light. Then he bandages my eye. Layers of bandages. I hear him talking to my parents. "Any deeper into the cornea and he would have been blinded. We'll wait a few days and see how he does."

These memories. They sneak up on me like assassins from the shadows. I stare back at my Red Wings and the memory goes away, back to those shadows where they lie in wait. The Red Wing shoes are up on the couch, where they belong, protecting me.

It's funny. Not funny I suppose, but curious. I look at the scuff marks on the Red Wings and they are identical on both shoes. How odd. A large scuff mark at the tips and smaller ones on the sides and insteps. The scuff marks are nearly white, with uncanny symmetry. How can they be the same on both shoes? How could both shoes have hit or brushed against objects in an identical way? Are they identical by design? Wait. Memories again. Symmetrical scuff marks. Those words, rearing up from memory- from a poem? "*What immortal hand or eye, dare frame thy fearful symmetry?*" Can it be random? Maybe they were chewed on by an intelligent animal. A rat. Or maybe a tiger. "*What dread grasp, dare its deadly terrors clasp?*"

It seems so natural. So settled. Observing those shoes. Watching, staring at them keeps the memories at bay. But not all the memories are bad.

I'm still a boy, but older- about eleven. It is October, my favorite month. Most of the memories of good things are in October. Outside, the wind blows and the trees are dancing. I remember being fascinated by the wind. Almost mesmerized. Innocence purifies sensation. I imagined the wind was generated by the trees. Those winds. When strong everything came alive. Street signs whipping in the air, frantic, insane. Leaves, litter, things not fastened, twisting in the whirl. I wanted the wind to come to me, to enter my pores and whisk me away.

Whoa-wait. How old am I, anyway? It seems I should know, at least within a few years. Judging by the wear and tear on my Red Wings, I've been around for awhile. I look up at them. In addition to the scuff marks, the soles are worn and flattened. And the laces. The laces are frayed, and might snap if tugged too hard. Such thoughts. It doesn't matter. I can't remember when I last felt a need to tie my shoes.

I hear something. A noise, a strange sound from outside. And is there a faint whiff of smoke? I suppose I should get up, but I'd only have to lay down again, so why bother? Why bother with anything? One of those great big philosophical questions. I've always wondered about stillbirths. Maybe some babies, fresh from the womb, take one look at the world and decide there's no point. Babies can be wise, their minds clear, uncorrupted by experience. They say only the strong survive. Maybe. Or maybe only fools survive, easily duped, not knowing what they're getting into. I've survived. And now I'm staring at my shoes.

That memory has come back. My eye still bandaged. I look at my sister. I observe her. She shows no guilt or shame. I have a father. A father seems all powerful when you're five. My father was cruel, like God. My sister had no sorrow, but she showed fear. If it was an accident, why was there never an apology? Would she be punished? No. She was my father's favorite, his adorable little princess. But something had to be done, did it not? He bought me a dog, and told my sister the dog was for me, and me alone. Years later, she confided that it was unfair that the dog was for me alone. The near blinding was never mentioned.

Where was I? Oh, I remember. My shoes. My Red Wing shoes. That other pair I have that's almost new. Isn't it time I made a change? Probably overdue. But the old ones, the ones I have on now, the ones I'm staring at this very moment, are so familiar. They're practically like old friends. How could I discard them, toss them aside, abandon them for a newer pair? That would be cruel. My father was cruel. I despise cruelty.

There's really something quite admirable about them. Those Red Wings. They show perseverance. Tenacity. I'm looking at them right now, propped up on the couch. They really do look their age, whatever that may be. They've taken quite a beating, but they're still here, right up on the couch. Listen to me. Describing how beat up they are, as if I had nothing to do with it. As if someone else steals them away at night, punishing them, wearing them down, running through ground glass, kicking at jagged rocks, rubbing them against the rough walls of decayed, abandoned buildings. I would never do that, treat them that way. They are old companions, and we should respect and cherish our old. But they are my shoes, only mine. I am the original and only owner, so I must be at least to some degree culpable for their condition. I have been derelict in their proper maintenance. I mustn't dwell on this, wallowing in guilt. My sister never felt guilt. Life must be easy, unencumbered by guilt or shame. Conscience is heavy, a heavy burden to bear. Living without conscience. Decisions must be easier, unambiguous, no second guessing. Not having a conscience must be like walking on air. I have a conscience. I must swear an oath to treat my shoes with greater respect. My shoes. My precious Red Wing shoes.

Oh yes. The dog. My sweet, loving comfort dog. Her name was Honeybee. She was a quiet, gentle Cocker Spaniel. She was my dog. Mine alone. Oh how she hated me for that. My sister, I mean, not of course Honeybee. Memories. Memories can kill, reminding us how horrible things can be. I wish I could kill the memories- the bad ones at least. Strangle them in the cradle, before they grow and become overpowering.

It was getting dark. I was outside, in the front yard. Fear was in the air, dread within the looming night. Where were they? My father was home, but the door was locked. My cruel father behind a locked door. My mother was out somewhere with my sisters. Oh, did I forget to mention there were two sisters? One was four years older than me, the one who nearly blinded my right eye, and the other was four years older than her. They were so much alike. Like Siamese twins who were born at different times. Why was I out alone in the night? Was I forgotten? Abandoned? I pounded on the door. Nothing. The night was black and I was cold. Where were the moon and stars? The sky was without hope. The sky was black like the night. I shivered. Where were they? Wait. There was a gate. Honeybee was behind the gate, and she could see me. She wanted to help me. But I had been told. Never, never open the gate, or Honeybee would run away. I remember. I wish I could strangle the memory, but it has survived too long outside the cradle, and it overpowers me. I open the gate. Honeybee runs past me, out to the street. There is a car. The car runs over Honeybee. She is dead.

I suppose it is a good sign that, an omen perhaps, that my Red Wing shoes look the same. The scuffs are not wider, the soles not thinner. I stare at them. I could stare at them forever.

And then came the bleeding from inside.

Time has passed. About five years? Yes, that's it. It was slow. Slowly evolving, insidious. I was tired. I felt unwell, but initially not sick. There were other boys in my neighborhood. They were all bullies. Some were brothers, or cousins. As I got sicker, their bullying escalated. Myths. We are taught many myths. There is the myth children are pure and gentle, and only change as they mature. Children can be vicious. My sickness made me weaker, and easier prey for the bullies. They were all older than me. One day three of them cornered me after it had rained. We fought. I hit back. One hit me and I fell into a puddle. They cheered in triumph. I went home and told my father. No father would allow three older boys to beat up his son who was younger and smaller. He laughed. I learned. I learned that if you are not strong and you have no one strong protecting you, then you are prey. I had no one protecting me but I have survived. Does that mean I am strong? Maybe. Or maybe I just slipped through the cracks.

When did I buy them? Not the newer ones, but the ones I'm wearing now? The scuffed ones. The battle scarred, world weary ones. I must have bought them. I know they weren't given to me. I've had very few gifts, or so goes my memory. These times- these moments are difficult. I'm trying to stitch things together, to reconstruct from memory. But memories are cruel and sometimes blurred, like fighting amidst the raindrops, like gazing through the tears.

There was one bully in particular. His name was Mike. He and his family moved in across the street and like a lion on the prowl he spotted me immediately, like a frightened gazelle with its ears sticking up. Like most bullies he wasn't cruel and abusive all the time, just most of the time. The one thing that may have made him a kindred spirit of sorts was that he also had an abusive father. He was a hulking man with a stiff leg who abused both Mike and his older brother Fred, who actually was a bit of a gentle giant. Oh how fickle are the apples falling from the tree, some stopping at the trunk's base, others rolling as if seeking escape. Mike was in the same grade as me, but had been held back a grade for undisclosed reasons. He was big and strong with thick bones- the ideal physique for a bully. Like many bullies, he tended to bully more when in the presence of others (why demonstrate one's ability to inflict pain and domination without an appreciative audience?)

One day after school as I was heading home Mike appeared down the street, waving his arms excitedly. He shouted, "Go to the Westmeyer's back yard-something bitchin' is going to happen!" Other boys from the neighborhood were also growing excited, and followed Mike. I knew. I knew that "something bitchin'" was code for something horrible. But I couldn't help myself and followed the throng to the Westmeyer's back yard.

A few months prior, the youngest of three of Westmeyer's sons had been given two baby chicks as a Christmas gift. Was it the era or the stars, but Mr. Westmeyer was also a cruel, in a decidedly Teutonic fashion, authoritarian brute. Ah yes, such an era, when a man was lord of his castle. Now the chicks had fully matured, and as I walked through the gate into the backyard I saw Mr. Westmeyer standing powerfully before a tree stump with a chicken in one hand and a large cleaver in the other. I often wondered if a majestic tree had been cut down with the sole purpose of providing a proper chopping block. A wave of nausea was welling up in my gut. It was even worse than I had imagined. The first chicken was placed neck down on the stump, and the cleaver came down. There was a loud squawk, and a headless chicken fell off the stump, flopping around for a moment before becoming still. I went into shock, prematurely, as the second beheading was far worse. The cleaver came down again, but this time the chicken's body was in denial, and began running around the yard like a, well, like a chicken with its head cut off. It ran and ran, with Mr. Westmeyer in grotesque pursuit, the chicken running and hopping until reality set in and the chicken, though headless, realized he was dead. I wondered, with child-like innocence, if the chicken's head watched his body running amok. And what of people? People during the French Revolution who were guillotined, heads falling into a basket. Was there still consciousness for a few moments, and did their headless bodies run and hop about for them to see? Ah poor Marie Antoinette, in those final moments, regretting her suggestion that the masses try carb loading before storming the Bastille.

My reaction to the hapless chickens seemed to inspire Mike's bullying endeavors to greater heights. Most of the other boys who bore witness to the decapitations did indeed seem to find the event bitchin'. But my shock and horror were the reactions of a sissy. There would be times when Mike would sneak up on me and throw me to the ground for no reason other than the sheer bliss of bullying. Once he approached me with a closed container which he opened and told me to take a whiff. Stupidly, I complied and nearly passed out on the suffocating fumes. It was pure chlorine Mike's father used for their swimming pool. Another time Mike snuck up on me at school during recess and got me in a choke hold. I remember beginning to blackout when the frantic voice of another boy rang out, "Stop-you're choking him!" Ah, the dearth of adult supervision in those good old days. Well, boys will be boys, won't they? Think of the joyous frolic of the young lads in *Lord Of The Flies*. Finally, after three years of bullying, I had the temerity to punch him in the face. Oh that cherished look of astonishment- of sudden fear. The worm had turned.

Mike and his family moved soon after (the odds of my punch being the catalyst are feeble.) Some years later I heard Mike was trying to get high by sniffing from an aerosol can of cocktail glass coolant. His lungs froze, and he suffocated. When he was found, he purportedly had regurgitated a portion of intestine in his struggle for breath. The intervention of karma is a tempting thought, but alas, sometimes horrible things also happen to horrible people.

But not all memories are traumatic. Here. Let me concentrate. Let me conjure a good memory, with an assist, of course, from my Red Wing friends.

I'm a bit older now, but still a boy. I think I'm twelve. I've learned to keep to myself. There is the world outside, the world of cruelty and misfortune. But there are other worlds, worlds inside the mind that cannot be breached by bullies and cruel fathers. By cars that run over innocent animals. By hateful sisters without guilt or shame.

One day- one beautiful October day, I was sitting alone beneath a tree, sheltered in one of my private worlds, when a girl approached me. She was older, but not that much. She greeted me and said her name was Toni. She was tomboyish, but pretty. Her hair was short and blond. Her clothes were worn, almost raggedy. She reminded me of Peter Pan. Whoa. Wait just a minute. Was Peter Pan a boy? I can't quite remember. On T.V., wasn't Peter Pan always played by a girl? Oh well, it doesn't really matter. Peter Pan or not, Toni was a girl.

Toni was friendly and flirtatious, and a bit aggressive. The fact that she seemed to appear from nowhere made her all the more fascinating. There was an abandoned house in the neighborhood. She led me to the house and we went inside. There was random clutter inside. Streams of light through a broken window met the dust inside, creating beams, white and ghostlike. Then Toni kissed me. She wanted to teach me. She kissed me on my lips, then her tongue went inside my mouth. I kissed her back the same way. I was a good student, better than I was in school. We kissed and it was good and outside it was October. We kept kissing and October came inside, riding on the streams of light. We met again during that magic month, hidden in our secret meeting place. I wish I could remember more, but that's where the memory ends.

They are advertised as work boots. The Red Wings. I've never understood that. They can be worn anywhere, not just work. And they're not boots. Boots ride high, between the ankle and the knee. That's not what they are. They're shoes. Who would know better than me? Not only do I wear them, but I stare at them all the time. I suppose that's an odd thing to do. Perhaps unnatural, aberrant behavior. Is it even behavior? I think of behavior as being active, involving movement of some sort. Even small subtle movements like nervous tics and neurotic yawning involve movement. But when I stare at those shoes, those Red Wing shoes propped up on the couch, I seem so passive. Totally immobile. What kind of behavior is that? There is good behavior and bad behavior. Yes, I realize that's an absurd over simplification. But for the time being just go with that. Good behavior is doing something positive, constructive. Bad behavior is doing something negative, destructive. This supposition certainly warrants further exploration at some point. Maybe later. But this is for sure- when I stare at my shoes I really am doing nothing. Nothing at all.

Getting back to the bleeding. I'm back to when I was ten, before it started. There were three brothers. Ray, the oldest, Bill the middle, and Mikey, who was my age. It was funny with Mikey. Sometimes he could be a bully, but most of the time we were friends. We were different. Mikey was wild, athletic, an impulsive risk taker. I was the opposite. Shy, withdrawn, apprehensive. I was the kid who couldn't make it over the wall when everyone else could. I was a slow runner and the last chosen for team sports. One day Mikey invited me to come over to his house after school to play football with him and his brothers. Tackle football.

Mikey teamed up with the oldest brother Ray and I teamed up with middle brother Bill. It was strange. They looked so much alike. Replicas of different sizes. Like in the Three Billy Goats story. They were of Irish heritage. Reddish blond hair. Freckles. I was darker. Italian heritage. Smaller. I had never played football before.

I got the ball. I was tackled on the spot. I watched the others play to learn what to do. I got the ball again. Tackled again, but I gained a yard. Then they had the ball and I was on defense. Mikey ran over me. But I got back up. The next time he came at me I got lower and put my shoulder into him. He went down. I felt exhilarated. And so it went. I was getting my ass kicked, but kicking ass back. I was gaining their respect and losing track of time. I couldn't wait to tell my father how well I had done. He would be so proud.

It didn't seem so late as I hurried home. It wasn't dark yet. There was a rule which was never shared with me that I was never to come home late without asking permission. When I reached home my sisters were on the front lawn, shaking with excitement. There was a glazed, glowing quality in their eyes. "You're in trouble- big trouble," my older sister stated. "I've never seen him this mad before!" stated the younger sister, with undisguised glee. They were terrible to behold. It was like being greeted by Cerberus, the three headed dog, before walking into Hades. There I go again. Greek myth. But it seems so appropriate. Tales of monsters, human and otherwise, horrible and tragic. Perfect for me.

I entered. He was waiting for me just inside the door. My mother stood next to him. Her eyes were like my sisters, gleaming. I knew at that point I was alone. His face was red, on fire like an enraged sun. Then, he removed his belt and began to beat me. I fell to the floor and assumed a fetal position as the belt cracked against my flesh. I thought it would never end. Soon after, within weeks, the bleeding inside me began.

The first thing you learn when you buy Red Wings is that they take forever to break in. Well, not literally forever. But it seems that way. At some point you might assume they are the wrong size and you are tempted to return them. Don't! If you're patient with them they will be patient with you. Eventually they will conform to your feet. They will be heavy and protective, but comfortable. They are loyal. I know, I'm personifying a pair of shoes. But sometimes those Red Wings have more humanity than most of humanity.

I wonder about memories. I have so many. Bad ones, so very few good ones. I wonder. I wonder if. I know this will sound crazy, but bear with me. What if we could change our pasts by changing our memories? I know I'm veering off into uncharted conceptual territory. What I'm about to suggest is hard to get a handle on. Even for me, and it's my idea. You've probably heard of the Time Traveler's Conundrum. Or maybe it's more of a paradox. Someone goes back in time and changes one tiny little thing, setting off a cause and effect revision of such exponential proportion that when the time traveler returns to the present everything is unrecognizable. It just goes to show how fragile reality is. And that's my point. Bullies. Bullies again, everywhere. Fate and Destiny are bullies. You know what they say about bullies when you stand up to them. They back down, cringe, crack and fold (actually, if you stand up to a bully, the chances of getting your ass kicked are excellent, for many bullies are strong and fearless, so once again what the proverbial "They" say should be taken with a grain of salt.) But for the sake of discussion let's say we are bullied and pushed around by Fate, Destiny and reality, and one day we push back and discover they are not all powerful. We discover they are pliable. Malleable. Putty in our hands. OK. I'm getting carried away. I admit it. But, for the sake of argument, let's assume Fate, Destiny and reality are not completely intractable.

And so a bad thing happens to us when we are children. Something tragic, brutal, unjust. And this event traumatizes us and is imprinted in our minds. Etched indelibly in our psyches. And as we grow up, from time to time the bad memory rears its ugly head. OK. Fasten your seat belts. Here it comes:

The bad memory is lucid, every detail clear as day. And. And here's the big what if. What if we consciously alter the details? Customize them. Reinvent them. Not all at once, but a detail or two at a time. And eventually the bad memory is reborn as a good one. And now it's a good memory indelibly etched into our psyches. Could we, if we became skilled at memory reconstruction, force reality's hand to change the past? And it wouldn't be like the Time Traveler's Conundrum because now the horrible traumatic event from the past becomes illusory. It never really happened in the first place! What really happened is I kicked ass playing football with the three Billy Goat brothers and swaggered home late, to be sure, but my sisters are nowhere to be seen on the front lawn and when I go inside the house my parents are relieved to see me and when I relate to them my victory my mother blurts, "Oh, I knew you would never come home late from school unless you were doing something truly magnificent!" And my father, face again red but now from beaming with pride, gives me a powerful, benevolent paternal bear hug and bellows, "Son, I'm so god damned proud I could explode with fatherly satisfaction!"

Well, anything is possible.

You've heard the expression "Walk a mile in my shoes?" Of course you have. I don't know why I'm even asking. It's a cliché, like "Beating around the bush," which everyone is familiar with and people say it all the time, but no one really knows what it means, just like no one knows "You get my goat." But I hear it all the time, usually from older people with rural roots. I always hated "You get my goat." Not just because of the inherent stupidity of the expression but because it's polarizing and educated urban people are contemptuous of people who use that expression because they stereotype and assume the sayers of that expression are ignorant Bible Belt bumpkins. Then the supposed bumpkins get contemptuous of the urban educated people because they are snotty snobby cosmopolitan elites looking down on the rural folks who are constantly muttering things like, "These liberals with their fancy book learnin'" but the reality is there are many conservatives with fancy book learnin,' like my all time favorite William F. Buckley Jr. who was even more of an elitist snob than most liberals. Uh oh. Did I stray off course? Did my sentences run away as they are wont to do when I'm on a roll? I was making reference to the expression, "Walk a mile in my shoes," and got distracted. But what if we all could walk a mile in each other's shoes? Well, I've got a hunch that in addition to getting blisters because everyone's feet are different the people who walked a mile in someone else's Red Wings would never want to return them to their proper owners that's how perfect and unique those wonderful shoes are. People never want to give them up. I know I never have and never would.

I guess I should get back to the bleeding I made reference to earlier. It's not polite to relate something to someone then not finish the story like some kind of tease. But it's painful. Not just the actual bleeding but describing the experience. Dredging up the memory, not that it needs dredging as the memory surfaces of its own volition. It lurks, lies in wait, never far from me. Here goes.

When I was ten I was a pudgy, unathletic kid who was indeed bullied. All of the kids in the neighborhood were older- luck of the draw. So much of life, good or bad, is luck of the draw, random. Roll the dice. For some people they roll sevens for others it's snake eyes every time. Not fair? Consider the other possibility. There is a guiding hand, pulling the strings on the marionettes of humanity, stacking the deck against some and paving the road to good health and fortune for others. Where was I? Oh yes, the bleeding. But I'll get back to that I know I'm meandering again but it's justified because I'm meandering into a deep philosophical question, one of the big ones that demands discussion and analysis. So let's begin with, what would be the worst scenario or possibility-random vs. guiding hand? Here are my thoughts:

In a random universe things might not seem fair but stop and think about it. Yes, some always seem to win the power ball lotto, the beauty queen contest, the most valuable player trophy, the Nobel Prize. Yes and it doesn't matter what behavior or character these perpetual winners display some literally, yes literally, with no hyperbole intended, have won the Nobel Peace prize by dropping bombs on civilians killing them by the millions and they say with nary shame nor sorrow that these massacres are to the benefit of humanity, the greater good for the greater number, for having massacred the millions it somehow prevented the massacre of billions by thwarting other wars and atrocities in the future. And they get away with it to the baaing bleating approval of the minions who never

question the absurd. They only see the shiny trophy or
Nobel plaque or whatever is handed out which of
course would never be awarded to someone who didn't
deserve it- would it? And, by the same token some live
hopelessly hapless lives and never win not because they
aren't diligent and virtuous and work hard but you see
it's random. They stumble on potholes break legs get
cancer watch indolent idiots in the workplace get
promoted over them they seem invisible in crosswalks
even random falling meteorites seem drawn to them for
they are perpetually in the cosmic crosshairs. But, all of
this is, ironically, perhaps perversely, fair <u>because</u> there
is no guiding hand. It's just stuff happening amidst an
infinity of stuff happening but the silver lining is it's
not to be taken personally!

So let's assume I was within the second category-
the hapless ones. A pudgy picked on kid picked on and
abused by both neighborhood bullies and sisters and
father alike. The kid who couldn't make it up the tree or
over the wall when all the others could, the kid who had
no allies advocates or protectors who one day was
struck with an inspiring idea: What if I could not fully
reinvent myself but at least remold both my body and
self-concept, become more fit and athletic? Just maybe
even more attractive to girls as puberty perhaps
uncharacteristically struck early for me and those pesky
little hormones were beginning to do acrobatics within
my endocrine system. And so began a self-

improvement regimen (please note I said *regimen* as opposed to *regime* one of the most pervasive misuses of language in our society perhaps most people feel exercise is so miserable it suggests something one would do within an oppressive regime this misuse drives me crazy but not, of course, nearly as much as "You get my goat") of diet and exercise, nothing extreme mind you, really just basic calisthenics and a few weight training movements with a pair of ten pound dumbbells. And lo and behold it seemed to work and I gradually became more athletic and accepted by my peers and less targeted by the bullies and I eliminated all junk food from my diet and the pudge melted away and who knows maybe through my self-motivational endeavors I was able to do myself proud against the before mentioned Billy Goat Brothers but then, as haplessness is, my father stepped in.

He was opposed to my self- improvement program and I mean vehemently opposed which I know sounds strange as you'd think most fathers would be proud as punch to see their pudgy weak unathletic sons take the bull by the horns and work diligently to become the kind of son who reflects positively on the manhood of the father because let's face facts fathers who have sired strong athletic sons strut and swagger because they feel it reinforces the sense of primordial power emanating from their loins.

But not my father. Was it a Freudian thing? Did he fear that by empowering myself that I would one day be strong enough to get Oedipal on his ass and torment him as he had tormented me like father like son like karma like what's good for the goose is good for the gander which is another obnoxious saying right up there with "You get my goat" or perhaps a rung or two lower? And I swear to you this is true honest injun' cross my heart one day he forced me to eat an entire fruit pie blueberry if I recall in front of my gleeful gloating sisters and you might be asking where was his mother during all this abuse? And the fact is I don't know she was there but again she wasn't.

I wonder at times if too much analysis is a bad thing? No not about the memories, the persistent memories of a traumatic childhood. I'm referring to my Red Wings the Red Wings that are a constant a rock an anchor keeping me from drifting into an abyss of madness. Some people have a favorite hat or jacket or pants or gloves and it's not a big thing. But these Red Wings are a big thing for me. I'm on my back on the couch and I'm staring up at them right now and somehow if I delve too deeply into why they are so significant it might in some way diminish their significance and yes we can all think too much but it may be better to quiet the mind and just accept something good in our lives especially if those good things are few and far between.

Did I mention my mother? Of course I did and not that long ago. Of late I've been thinking of her a great deal. I loved my mother deeply but was she really a great mother or seemingly so when compared to the other members of the family? I suppose we all do the best we can or so the saying goes we do our best under the circumstances an excuse, a rationalization, an out, circumstances beyond our control mitigating circumstances had the circumstances been just a little bit different then things events lives would have turned out differently. Or so they say.

My mother's mother or my grandmother if you prefer died when my mother was two a long time a very long time ago or so it seems as I'm not always sure what time it is myself. Not just the minutes, hours, days, but months or even years. My grandmother died during a catastrophic pandemic. It could have been a hundred years ago or yesterday as it seems history in its most horrific hours persists and repeats itself as we gawk at the horror of our time we should have seen it coming perhaps we did but our souls were leaden weighed down by docility and dumb inertia.

These memories. Sometimes they are so lucid like I'm watching something right in front of me in real time whatever the hell that means it suggests certain times are less authentic than others but don't let me wander yank hard on my leash before my train of thought plummets off the rails. Other times the memories are more opaque wrapped in gauze elusive to the mind and senses.

My mother or mom as I always called her except when I was a little tyke and called her mommy and how odd it is how few of us men call our mothers mother it sounds overly formal effete and pretentious for a full grown man to refer to his mother as mother as in, "Hello mother, how are you today?" or, "It would be wonderful to have lunch with you on Sunday, mother," although I must say it does seem that upper crust Englishmen can get away with it, although it sounds more like "Mutha" when they say it and a few even say, "Mumsy" which requires skill and finesse in order to not get beaten up by some Cockney cab driver. Look at me. There's a reason digression rhymes with obsession.

My mother was not perfect. One of her glaring imperfections was marrying my father, but we all make mistakes and to err is human and some of us radiate humanity by the degree and frequency of our errors. But she was very loving and caring when the bleeding inside escalated and I was in the hospital for six weeks in a teaching hospital which is an insulting euphemism for charity ward. My father was a successful real estate broker and we lived in a nice house so one might ask why was I in a charity ward? Because my father never

bought health insurance for his family and I remember
before I was admitted a young gastroenterologist came
to our home to observe the extent of my illness and I
swear I'm not making this up but his name was Dr.
Judge and he looked at our house and expensive
furnishings and with an expression of absolute
contempt looked at my father and said, "You have a
boy with ulcerative colitis and you have no health
insurance?" and for the first time in my life I saw my
father cringe not with shame but fear that he might get
called out on his financial status by the hospital and I
saw another grown man put my father in his place and I
knew he was a coward.

And I remember that I had a temperature of 105
degrees and was rushed to the hospital and for some
reason there was an argument on the hospital steps as to
whether I should be admitted. A woman doctor argued
against admittance but was finally overruled by a higher
ranking man and I nearly bled out on the hospital steps
and was immediately given a series of blood
transfusions upon admittance and I never knew why
there was reluctance to admit me was it my father's
financial status or perhaps admitting a gentile into a
Jewish hospital was not deemed, well, kosher.

And I soon learned I was not so much a patient as I
was a cadaver with a pulse and an object by which the
young cold interns could hone their skills which I

suspect were skills by which to turn a buck let's face reality they don't want us dead and they don't want us healthy neither condition of which draws a profit- they want us perpetually ill so we can be continuously cropped and milked like cows with our udders attached to milking machines.

Six weeks of fear and agony and countless blood transfusions and at one point there was discussion of a colostomy but something happened maybe they couldn't assemble the desired crew of early twenty somethings who had never touched a scalpel in their lives and when they could no longer learn from or make use of me I was released looking like a prisoner from Auschwitz and they told my parents during a discharge examination that the nickel sized sores on my lower back oozing blood and pus were a side effect of cortisone but in fact they were bed sores from patient neglect and oh how I hope everyone of them is burning in Hell but I survived and one day I purchased my first pair of Red Wings.

Did I mention how durable they are? They're like underpinnings of stability stalwart dependable incapable of treachery or betrayal slander assault atrocious manners boorishness or condescension. Is personification inappropriate? I say nay because most people lack the above virtues but on the other hand are rich in the afore named foibles. And if I haven't already mentioned it when you buy a pair included with the purchase are free leather treatments and lifetime shoelace replacements which is really quite remarkable considering their exceptional longevity. Ha! I sound like a Red Wing pitch man but nothing could be further from the truth. I'm a horrible salesman and couldn't sell popsicles to the damned my sincerity precedes me and I despise pitchmen especially over-the-hill celebrities who hawk life insurance and reverse mortgages and catheters for Christ's sake you'd think that after years of regular work in movies and T.V. they would have quite a nest egg but maybe bad investments drug or gambling addictions have left them bankrupt but I like to think the best of humanity so they're probably motivated by greed and a sincere belief that people are basically stupid and will buy anything touted by a familiar face and trusted voice.

Ulcerative colitis is an autoimmune disease. That is when someone's immune system goes wacko and attacks their own organs in this case the large intestine. There are triggers which can activate the disease and although causality is difficult to nail down there does seem to be a correlation between child abuse and ulcerative colitis UC for short. I first became symptomatic a couple of months after my coming home late from school beating. But the verbal abuse was by far worse, the constant attack on my self-esteem. My father was Sicilian and reveled in calling me "Stupido" he called me that far more than he ever called me by my real name. Sometimes when he was in a more congenial mood he would shorten it to "Stupe" as in "Where's the Stupe?" Undermining me and bowling were his two favorite hobbies in that order. Whenever I would attempt something new he was always there to admonish me with, "You can't do that, Stupido!" and oh such delight for my sisters, his adoring cheerleaders, his chorus his rooting section and I'm haunted truly haunted that I lacked the temerity to tell him before he died how much I truly hated him and having him as my father was worse than no father at all.

I wonder if it's Zen? The staring at my Red Wings I mean. I stare and stare with my feet propped up on the couch and stare and soon I become contemplative. Such an odd way to become contemplative others I'm sure stare at candles or perhaps things in nature brooks trees mountains rock formations they control their breathing all to achieve an altered state. I do nothing like that it's not a discipline I just put my feet up and stare at my shoes I don't chant ohm or any of that Eastern stuff that some people find so seductive and probably pay billions of dollars each year for courses taught by swamis or gurus who were once used car salesmen and I don't mean that as a blanket condemnation of gurus swamis or even used car salesmen. Everyone has to do something to earn a living except perhaps parasitic trust babies and I suppose it's unfair that selling used cars has become a metaphor for sleaze sham and dishonesty I mean someone's got to do it not everyone has the means to buy new cars. The fact of the matter is I have more respect for used car salesmen (or women for that matter although I've never actually seen one or gender fluid binary people although they may be more difficult to identify) than the swamis and gurus who fleece naïve people with a plethora of esoterica they're as bad as the disgusting televangelists hopping around on stage with bibles wedged up their asses. All of the poor people who can't afford to give these con men or should I say con persons are grasping, grasping for love hope and healing, these poor desperate people living miserable poor desperate lives and they long to be saved and loved from above. Did I neglect to mention the Fakirs those ascetic holy men are they Islamic or Hindu or a little bit of both? I like their name it sounds like Faker which can be applied to the entire lot of them regardless of creed which rhymes with greed. You should never worship anyone and even exercise moderation in expressing respect. It's so simple for me- no spiritual guide no middleman no chanting no passing the hat or tithing just staring simple honest staring at those simple honest Red Wings and I'm on my way. And oh, for you searchers out there puzzling over the unanswerable question, "What is the sound of one hand clapping?" One peek at my Red Wings and I've got the answer. It's the exact same sound as two hands clapping, only half as loud.

I wonder about the odds. The odds of some other guy out there out anywhere who wears Red Wing shoes and had a brutal sadistic father? One in a thousand? One in a million? One in a trillion? What if I'm all alone in this? It's OK- I'm used to being alone.

Memories. With memories come regret. Regret for things you've done and for things you should have done but didn't because of cowardice, insensitivity or worse- because of sloth and lethargy, of mind and spirit. Guilt is a curse. But people who have it are better than people who don't. Easier to traverse life without guilt, however, to glide without hesitation, second thoughts, considerations, encumbrances- no looking back, no remorse. The lightness- it must be like walking on air. But with guilt comes conscience. These damn memories. They haunt like relentless ghosts. I remember her. She's forever in my heart and head and won't go away. Her name was Carol.

I've mentioned them. Those bullies of my neighborhood. For them, I wasn't enough. Always on the prowl, a jackal pack seeking prey everywhere, searching for a vulnerable victim; someone to hurt, humiliate and traumatize. Poor, innocent Carol.

There was a ramshackle old house. Carol's house. It was in the middle of a large open field. This is the

house where the poor people lived- Carol and her
family. Poor people. The poor the honest poor who
occupy their social stratum usually through
circumstance and not lack of virtue or work ethic the
working poor the shunned poor the pariah poor poor
people like lepers who have wandered from their
colony despised by the rich and perhaps more by the
middle class. Poor. They remind those who are not poor
that all is not right in our society that one false move
and they too could be poor and the poor are powerless
unless organized and they can be bullied and abused
like Carol was.

Carol and her younger sister Eileen were pretty
girls. Eileen was about ten, and Carol about twelve, and
they stood out at school because they wore hand me
downs. They looked like they were from another era,
like Dust Bowl children but they were clean and smart
and well behaved and they both had red hair and
freckles and blue eyes that sparkled.

The open field with the ramshackle old house
where the sisters lived with their parents was at the
front end of a cul de sac, a fancy euphemism for dead
end but this was no ordinary dead end, but an exclusive
private street and oh such a contrast a blighted glorified
shack diminishing the custom houses on our exclusive
street. This street where I lived was considered affluent
but that didn't provide me immunity from being an

outcast and Carol and I, though we rarely spoke, were kindred spirits.

Across the open field where Carol's house stood was another open field with a large tree with a rope swing and one day after a rain a large puddle pooled beneath the rope. Carol walked, or more correctly, ventured across the street and sat, with carefree nonchalance, on the swing. She looked so innocent in her vintage dress. She was pure and gentle, and she deserved kindness and respect. Then the bullies arrived.

There was Mike of chicken decapitation fame and Dave and his cousins Kenny and Michael the trio who had ganged up on me and knocked me into a puddle; the irony-the cruel repetitive irony. They surrounded Carol and began taunting her telling her she was White Trash and wasn't good enough to play on our side, their side, of the street and it escalated and they pushed her into the puddle and her shoes came off and Mike the strongest and most sadistic of the lot took one of her shoes and filled it with mud and Carol was crying and frantic and I was off to the side not knowing what to do- afraid, passive, do something do something the screaming voice inside repeated over and over again, hating the bullies and hating myself for doing nothing, when an adult arrived. It was Mr. Woods, a principal at one of the nearby schools. He and his family lived at the end of the cul-de-sac in one of the nicer of the nice homes and he was coming home from work and saw what was happening and stopped. He got out of his car and appraised the situation while approaching the commotion. Then he saw it was Carol who was being abused. He became livid and joined the bullies and shouted at her to go back to where she belonged and Carol ran home carrying her shoes crying traumatized humiliated and why was it like this why couldn't I be big and brave enough to stop what happened and on that day I saw authority for what it was in the form of Mr. Woods and I hated authority- just another kind of bully beneath a façade of legitimacy.

Maybe life turns in circles like a merry-go-round without an operator and we repeat events and lives cross paths again at some point and if I get another chance with Carol I'll take the beating I'll take the death I think of her every day of my life I want her to know I need her to know how sorry I am I should have done something Carol I should have at least approached you later when we would both be safe for at least a few moments if only I could have held you and felt your tears blend with my own.

I'm back. I'm back with my loadstar. My Red Wings. When the bad memories lead me down to the darkest path I refocus. They're solid unfaltering the same today as they were yesterday and dog gone it they'll be the same tomorrow. They're not subject to whims changing tastes mores fads trends subjective spins and frivolous revisionism. My Red Wings are my soul mates my best friends forever, my blood brothers immune to infidelity what would that even be like I can't imagine can't picture them flying off and enveloping another man's feet because that other guy has more appealing arches ha! an arch rival or sexier heels or takes more walks providing the shoes with much needed fresh air abandoning me because we never go anywhere. No no indeed they're not <u>that</u> kind of shoes and I would never abandon them because I'm not <u>that</u> kind of boy.

I think I need a happy memory or at least a positive one a memory to even things out but there will never be evenness because that is not the nature of things. But I must try.

I found one! It's a memory of a movie I saw as I was recuperating from my six weeks of hell in the "teaching hospital." My illness taught me something about healing. If you can escape from yourself and enter a different world a world of fantasy and imagination it's almost an out-of-body experience. You can vacate the sick body and define yourself as healthy, at least for a little while.

The movie. The movie that took me away from myself was *The Pit And The Pendulum* based ever so loosely on the immortal short story by Edgar Allan Poe, directed by Roger Corman and starring the sublime Vincent Price. Vincent Price so smooth suave yet sinister played a character named Nicholas Medina who is a Spanish don and lives in a sprawling Gothic Surrealistic castle overlooking the ocean. The opening scene shows Nicholas' brother-in-law Francis Barnard played by John Kerr being taken by carriage and left by the terrified carriage driver some distance from the castle and the opening scene of him trudging across the shore against the backdrop of the ocean the tumultuous foreboding ocean battering against the rocks as Francis walks toward the looming castle all spires and turrets dark with malevolence. It is 16th century Spain during the Spanish Inquisition and Francis has travelled from his native country England to investigate the silence of his sister Elizabeth played by the sinister and ethereally beautiful Barbara Steele and learns upon arrival that she has died suddenly of an illness but we soon learn that she didn't die initially but had catalepsy and Nicholas fears that she may have been entombed alive and Nicholas, Francis, Nicholas' sister played by the wonderful Luana Anders as Donya Medina and the family doctor Dr. Leon played by the obscure Anthony Carbone go to Elizabeth's tomb with picks and break through the bricks and force open the coffin and they all freak when they discover a putrescent corpse mouth agape with horror and broken hands that had been desperately pushing against the coffin from within and it was the most shocking horrifying image I had ever seen. But the plot thickens as Nicholas hears Elizabeth calling out to him and he hears her play the harpsichord and slowly he is being driven mad by guilt that he had buried alive the love of his life and when he finally snaps we learn that she is not dead but has plotted with her lover Dr. Leon and then the movie itself descends into madness as Nicholas believes he is his father who was a notorious inquisitor and all are forced down into the dungeon where his father's torture chamber has been collecting dust and Francis is tied to a table beneath a slowly descending pendulum with an immense blade and he is saved in the last minute after Elizabeth has been locked into an Iron Maiden type cage and Nicholas has been pushed into the pit below the pendulum dead from the fall and Francis and Donya Medina along with a loyal family servant decide the torture chamber shall be locked forever more and the movie ends with the image of Elizabeth her eyes bursting with horror and screaming locked forever in the cage a tomb of her own making.

But you see I had been absorbed by the movie by its story and atmosphere and removed from my sick self and placed into a state of pure wonder and imagination. Power. The power of art. The power of imagination and after watching *The Pit And The Pendulum* I fell in love with Edgar Allan Poe and read all of his stories and poems and I watched all of Roger Corman's movies based on the Poe stories although in truth most of them were based loosely and *The Pit and The Pendulum* the loosest of all and except for the actual pit and the pendulum and the time period the movie has nothing to do with the story on which it is based but who cares in the realm of the imagination license is unlimited and non sequiturs are as valid as the relevant.

Well, I'm back- back in the now as my Red Wings return to focus upon my gaze upward they're there exactly where they should be propped up on the couch not by themselves but enclosing my feet of course. Centered. That's what they do for me they keep me centered grounded anchored tethered moored to some semblance of reality of sanity- sanity that thing that state of mind on which my grip has always been tenuous my connection dubious my perception precarious.

What exactly is sanity? Is it subjective- subject to majority rules? Example: You're in an auditorium filled with a thousand people watching a ballet the lithe beautiful ballerinas twirl elegantly en pointe and the handsome muscular danseurs or ballerinos or whatever the hell the males are called perform preternaturally athletic leaps and you're transfixed by the extreme physical and aesthetic capacity of the human machine when the man sitting next to you nudges you in the ribs and whispers, "Absolutely amazing what those warthogs on stage are capable of- their animal trainers are ingenious." And you look at him and reply, "Warthogs? Are you insane? Those are human beings performing on stage," to which he replies, "No, no my good man, those are warthogs, highly trained warthogs." And you wonder if it's safe sitting next to a delusional lunatic when a man sitting in front of you turns to his wife and says, "Sweetheart, the warthogs are magnificent tonight," and she replies, "Yes dear, why they're almost human," and now you, the sane man, are outnumbered three to one it's uncanny what are the odds that three delusional people sitting near you have the same delusion when you spot a program on the floor and pick it up and it says, "Swan Lake, As Performed By The Royal Warthog Ballet," and now you're having doubts and when the first act ends the entire audience gives a standing ovation screaming "Bravo warthogs!" and now you are perceptually outnumbered a thousand to one so now who's the lunatic, Mr. Smarty Pants?

There have been times when I'm actually afraid to avert my eyes from my Red Wings. For when I do there is a sense of not just disorientation but in fact disintegration of losing identity and not knowing who or where or what I am and I may wander off into the void. Identity. Who am I really? For that matter who is anybody? Do we really know and is who we think we are the same as how others see us? The difference might be so great that if we could see ourselves through the eyes of others what we see might be unrecognizable. Consider if you will photos of yourself on your driver's license, passport, selfies etc. and there is a consistency. Oh sure your hair will not be the same in each picture or your facial expressions may vacillate but you can still recognize the essential you it's not like in one picture you have dark eyes and short dark hair then in the next you have long red hair and beard then in another you look twenty but in another you look ninety no the pictures are recognizably you with perhaps slight variance. But if we were to directly confront others and ask what they see they may reply, "Why, you have three eyes of course two brown and one blue and a single long horn on the top of your head and oh that wonderful smile." Or, "You look like a dignified horse's ass made all the more distinguished by that wagging tail protruding from your nose." Who knows who really knows how we are perceived oh well as long as I don't look like a warthog.

Reconnect. Time for reconnection before going off on these tangents which take me to the edge the very edge of the earth where people who fall off are never seen from again thus shattering the myth held by Round Earthers and their gullible fellow travelers. This is not a frivolous thought. A basic question: should the wandering mind be corralled or given full reign? Pros and cons on both. Police powers a curfew of sorts do not go beyond this line your thoughts are part of your personal sovereignty which stops when they tell you to stop. A speed limit on thinking slow down or stop violators will be prosecuted. Or perhaps total freedom Laissez Faire let the chips fall where they may we warned you now suffer the consequences.

Memories again. None are linear. Why are most so horrible? Perhaps nightmares by virtue of their intensity are simply more memorable than pleasant dreams. Or, sadly, there may simply be more nightmares. Shouldn't there be a law of averages a bell shaped curve a yin and yang heads or tails it's all out of balance the deck is stacked there but for the grace of randomness go I or for that matter you.

First day of first grade. Recess. Hordes of kids throngs of them playing on the cold grey blacktop such an odd grammar school no grass not a blade and the adult supervisors stand frozen statues they watch but they do not see they may as well be props department store mannequins or scarecrows that are pecked at by contemptuous crows. I'm standing alone. I'm scared. I seem to be the only boy who is not connected to a pack. The other boys run about in violent chaos then four of them spot me. They approach happy and smiling and ask me a question. I can't remember what the question was or if I answered, then, in the blink of an eye, they grab me and force me to my knees down onto the blacktop. Two of them hold my arms and the other two lift my head and slam my forehead down against the blacktop. In a dizzy blur I see tetherballs in the background swirling out of control. They lift me up I'm crying a large goosebump swells on my forehead I run and tell a teacher or monitor or some adult authority what happened she laughs not gleefully but nervously as if to say, "Well, what to you expect me to do about it?" I'm alone. Alone and standing in shock when another boy appears a friend of the others and he looks at my bump and begins to laugh uproariously and I reflexively punch him in the face then he begins to cry and runs off then he returns with his friends they're about to come at me again then the bell rings. But the horror of this grassless school doesn't end there.

There was a girl. A little Black girl. I don't recall any other Black children in the entire school. One day during recess there was commotion beyond the usual pandemonium. There was an enraged, rabid circle of White kids surrounding the Black girl. They were screaming at her. The voice of one White boy resonates and echoes to this day. "We don't want you going to school here because you're a nigger!" The look on her face. Crimson blending with black. The spectrum- the rainbow of emotion on that child's face: fear, hurt, rage, then resolve and finally strength bolstered by pride. Once again; why couldn't I have done something? Where were the adults, invisible and duplicitous by their indifference? I always wondered what happened to her. Soon after that day, she was gone. Both of us were soon gone.

I can't harbor these memories for long they remind me of the horror the injustice the brutality of life and madness begins to sniff like the wolf at the door snap out of it refocus on the Red Wings displacing dogs of all breeds as man's best friend or at least this man's best friend or more properly friends as they are a pair.

It's funny. I never really researched or asked questions about my Red Wings maybe because I can't remember buying them. It's almost as if they emerged from the womb at the same time I did. Or they may have popped into existence like Athena popping spontaneously out of her father Zeus' head. Mythology again. I make references to Greek Mythology often and why not the Greek myths are highly relevant the Gods and Goddesses just like us only more so talk about bullying ask Atlas or Sisyphus or especially Prometheus being tormented for eternity for one minor slight one false move look at poor Prometheus no good deed will go unpunished introducing fire to a freezing humanity **How Dare Him!** No time off for good behavior no reduced sentence commute or pardon no thirty days in Hades then released because you've done your time learned your lesson been successfully rehabilitated paid your debt to Olympian Society and boy from now on I'll mind my p's and q's. Uh uh. No, you're consigned to eternal laceration of the flesh and spirit Prometheus my champion the champion of Shelly and the Romantic poets you saved humanity but defied Zeus so as punishment you are tied to a mountain and every day an eagle will swoop down and eat your liver which grows back the next day and the eagle swoops down again ad infinitum but always your liver regenerates and if only people who need liver transplants had this capacity sans eagle and eternal torment people could drink all they want and not worry about cirrhosis.

I wonder. I wonder about these memories. I wonder if dreams and fantasies interact with memories in some symbiotic way. I have recurring dreams I have them over and over again well of course I do that's why they're called recurring. One. One in particular. It's a dream with variations that's evolved into a kind of fantasy. Here goes: I'm in a battlefield with a group of other men. We're treading softly, cautiously with walking on eggs trepidation advancing toward the enemy there are trenches and barbed wire bent and mangled throughout the landscape and smoke permeating dark billowing smoke acrid and ominous. Then. Then the shelling begins. The battlefield becomes pocked with craters from the shelling and a sense of dread and panic envelopes us all and my comrades begin to fall around me and soon I will join them when a shell lands beside me and I'm thrown into a crevice in the ground shaken and shocked but not injured a crevice a cavity a nook where I'm protected from the carnage surrounding me I can lift my head and through a crease I can see the horror of battle the horror of the world but I am safe I am exempt within this natural womb Mother Earth has fortuitously provided confined and given refuge and salvation. And here's the oddness the irony the experience is not frightening nor do I feel guilt that I have been chosen selected anointed as the others around me lie dead or dying the experience is calming peaceful almost pleasurable Lady Luck has taken a shine to me and damn it it's about time.

I'm back. Back again, contemplating my Red Wings. Yes, not just staring or gawking which diminishes and vulgarizes my intimate interactions with my beloved friends and footwear but indeed contemplating with respect and adoration like in the great 17th century painting by Rembrandt *Aristotle Contemplating A Bust Of Homer* deferring to them just as Aristotle defers to Homer. Am I unreasonable even irrational to harbor these thoughts this elevation literal and figurative of my shoes I can see how easily my sentiments might be dismissed as obsession fixation or fetish but humor me just a bit if people can be idolatrous of monuments statues totems shrines talismans inanimate things large and small then why not raise a pair of fine old shoes to lofty if indeed not celestial heights? People are judgmental and ego-centric seeing black and white and redacting grey, reality is complex and nuanced and there are gradations and continuums it won't fit in a nutshell and never forget one man's idol may very well be another man's shoe.

Memories. Another memory appears peeking and poking inside my head what is it this time? Ah I'm brought back a child again during a period of respite from the trauma and dread I may be nine or there about I smell the ocean salt and seaweed blended with the aroma of corndogs hamburgers beer sweat and funk yes funk from the sea, funk from the human cavalcade within a place, an amusement park called the Pike. I loved the Pike. It was more of a home than home it was so real and happy and sad the polar opposite of the homogeneous sterile vanilla Happiest Place On Earth I needn't say the name you know the place I mean that plastic happy goofy phony place I always despised and rightfully so. But not the Pike. I remember a man standing next to the roller coaster he looked like a Neanderthal they would say he was ugly in the Happiest Place. He held his infant son who looked identical to his father a fragile replica the boy is crying and his cries are mirrored by his father's tears they sob together in synch the empathy a father's love and empathy humanity sad humanity at its best. The Pike. An education and epiphany for an innocent young boy innocent except in knowing suffering except in having compassion and tendrils that reach far and connect with the suffering of the world and that's what the Pike was a microcosm of the world without sugarcoating a panorama of humanity my kind of humanity a parade of sailors hustlers pimps prostitutes you can't have one without the other or so insist the pimps a panoply of outcasts of interracial couples which I had never seen before, of the disfigured and disabled, the proud and the shamed, the pitchmen and patched women, scarred but not beaten beautiful in their imperfection the queer yes it's OK to say queer now or so I've been told they were accepted everyone accepted under the big tent the three ring circus and lest I forget the freaks my favorite of them all turning deformity and tragic fate into a divine art oh how I loved you all at first sight for many reasons not the least of which is none of you would ever be allowed to set foot in The Happiest Place On Earth.

I suppose one can argue that at some point if we live long enough we are our memories as much as our memories are us the less we actively experience life the more life becomes an archive a vault a capsule of memories memories of things past but ponder if you will or if you can this: what if we can also have memories of things future things that may never happen but should happen if we were at the helm of our own destiny? Think of the power. Think of the freedom. Self-fulfilling prophets of our own fate. If only. If only it could be.

How did this come to be? A pair of shoes albeit magnificent ones becoming my focal point my north star my sextant dare I say it my best friends? Oh how pitiful that must sound! What does that say about me as a man as a human being as a member of society or for a more positive twist what does it say about the Red Wings that they can demand such loyalty respect affection reverence devotion from their wearers or if universality is a stretch from one wearer namely me. But they <u>must </u>have some magic some aura essence magnetism mojo I once stared at my cuffs for hours nothing nada like a party with no guests like a séance boycotted by the spirits snubbed by the dearly departed dog gone there's something about those shoes.

There are those among us who believe in reincarnation and déjà vous. And indeed as alluded to earlier memories may be layered like a city built upon ancient ruins which in turn were built upon earlier ruins we return to memories or they return to us edited embellished diluted mercurial and dynamic. I have memories elusive ephemeral memories in which I can't remember the events that spawned the memories. I remember and visualize myself as a different person in a different time but that person in basic essence is me. Reincarnation? Imagination? Perhaps both perhaps neither. An example: It's summer. Several years before I was born. I'm young healthy handsome well built a bodybuilder when bodybuilders were looked upon as freaks and remember to me being perceived as a freak is the highest form of flattery. I live in Coney Island or Santa Monica probably Santa Monica circa early nineteen fifties. I work out during the day lifting weights the effort and effect are exhilarating the pump the sweat the sense of power when finished I languish on the beach important to have that tan. Indolent? Narcissistic? Not contributing to society? Perhaps. I live in a small apartment near the beach. Source of income? Ambiguous. Am I a model perhaps or do I do occasional construction jobs enough to get by utilize my strength in a practical way? Nights. Summer nights. There is a small bar or café within walking distance from my apartment a cool place where the hip people the Beat Bohemian Bongo people the poets jazz musicians visionaries luminary lunatics outlaw outcast pariah people my people hang out. And exotic women. Scary women. Beautiful viper women in black leotards they dance to the jazz jerk to the bongos sensual slithering dancing ancient dancing demonic serpentine dancing primal pre-Christian Pagan dancing primordial conjuring dancing the kind of dancing that pleases the Devil and teases the saints and they look upon me and their eyes roll up and down my body and the moon is full and the night is hot and nothing will ever be better than this or maybe…

Sometimes I feel like I'm on drugs lassitude inducing drugs when I stare at and contemplate my Red Wings externals go into hiding and time loses credibility meaning purpose perhaps those shoes are all that there is perhaps <u>they are the primal atom</u> containing all the matter and energy in the universe as opposed to some microscopic dot in the inky void.

There was a song. Summer again. I stare out the window at the steamy night I'm thirteen or so and the radio is on as I lay in bed. *Sally Go Round The Roses*. The song haunts. What does it mean? *Sally go round the roses, Sally go round the pretty roses. Roses they can't hurt you, no the roses they can't hurt you.* What is it about that song? A simple pop song but the sense of foreboding and creeping ritual the strange rhythm and repetition I was transfixed *Sally don't you go, don't you go downtown- saddest thing in the whole wide world, is to see your baby with another a girl.* Why did this song affect me so and in such a way this sense this terrible sense that at any moment the ax will come down *They won't tell your secret, no the roses won't tell your secret- Sally baby cry, let your hair hang down, sit and cry where the roses grow, you can sit and cry not a soul will know.* Why has this song latched onto me never letting go sometimes out of the blue it will creep and insinuate inside my head take root what secret Sally share your secret with me is this one way madness takes hold obsession fixation *Sit and cry where the roses*

grow sit and cry not a soul will know over and over
again it reverbs inside my head round and round tell me
Red Wings what did Sally know? Murder where the
roses grow or the insanity of lost love lost everything
speak, spill, whisper some clue but my dearest Red
Wings like Easter Island heads stare back silent and
inscrutable.

There was a rat. Some years back but not that long
ago. I remember. It was hot very hot September my
sliding glass balcony door pulled open the screen had a
hole in it not large but large enough for a rat to crawl
through and I saw him meander casually through the
hole then he disappeared into some shadowy nook or
cranny. A rat. What is it about rats? We are afraid
repulsed disgusted by rats I saw a rat I think I smell a
rat you better not rat on me dirty no good rat bearers of
bubonic plague quick call the exterminator where's the
Pied Piper when we need him? Are we unreasonable?
Irrational? Overreactive to these creatures the rodent
cohabiters of ours? Within the urban jungle they've
been around longer than us far more versatile and
ubiquitous than we they thrive everywhere in the
sewers up in the trees in the basements attics barns bins
holes cracks outer limits and inner sanctums on all
continents well I'm not sure about Antarctica but we
don't exactly thrive there ourselves so don't get smug
all you arrogant upright bipeds. Ah. Irony.
Inconsistency. Consider this, rebut it if you can but you

can't squirrels yes squirrels are also rodents urbanized like Brother Rat so very similar gnawing devouring our gardens our orchards they too are harmful but we are not repelled repulsed revolted sickened or alarmed by the little rascals those big brown eyes those cute bushy wiggly tails we adore them feed them nuts how endearing standing on their hind legs nibbling on the treats we provide oh can't you just pick one up and hug it and coo and smile and say, "Who's a good squirrel" with that embarrassing dopey tone we have when we talk to our beloved dogs?

It was a large rat dark grey in color and I was on pins and needles he was there in my home somewhere he could see me but I could not see him I had closed the sliding glass door thinking more rats might come inside an invasion an infestation I'm outnumbered what dread fate might be in store for me why they're capable of anything they might gang up on me famished rodents I am rather succulent delectable if I say so myself downright scrumptious a buffet of body parts for my rodent guests I could imagine them glutting themselves down to my marrow picking their teeth with my bones then departing without leaving a tip. But that didn't happen. I could see him in my room see his shadow running amok and morphing each new time I would see him, fleetingly, through the corner of my eye. He seemed larger with each new sighting and the irony is that he was probably trying to get out and had I left the screen door open he probably would have departed and this tale would have a happier ending.

I contacted a rodent exterminator/relocator a pleasant young fellow he arrived and examined my abode impressed with the plethora of rat droppings adorning my floor he and his little dog Frankie who he explained was bred to, perhaps ironically, ferret (another rodent!) out rats and dispatch them by shaking them to death and I explained I would prefer to have the rat evicted so he set up three humane traps, cages where the rat would enter and the door would snap shut so Mr. Rat could be spirited away safely and humanely and I'm not sure why but he also set up three kill traps you know the kind the time honored back breaking snap traps why both it seemed almost literary *The Lady Or The Tiger* a true O'Henry scenario who knows perhaps he was placating me and the humane traps were dummies for show only to appease skittish old ladies and wussy guys like myself and I couldn't take it I couldn't bear to hear a kill trap snap shut breaking the silence of the night what if it was not a clean kill and the darkness shattered by the pitiful screams of an agonized living creature so I checked into a hotel for the night and when I returned home in the morning I found him he chose the tiger the kill trap and I felt ambivalence relief and remorse and I picked up the trap rat and all with a shovel and placed him in a plastic bag and put him in the dumpster and I could almost hear my father's voice bellowing with contempt for the squeamish gutless son he had spawned and maybe he would be right.

Lethargy left unchecked exerts a strong and insistent gravitational force. I'm staring up at them as I lay inert on the couch. Staring up at the Red Wings, propped up on their usual place up on the couch's back, left ankle crossed over on the right. Should I lift my leg and place the right ankle over the left? Newton. A body at rest tends to stay at rest. Should I buck the system the cosmic system and switch positions on my Red Wings which tend to stay at rest? Initiate change in a static stagnant universe, push gravity, smug gravity, aside and give Newton second thoughts, self-doubt, some much needed humility make him regret the apple fell on his head the apple never falls far from the tree so he must have been hugging the trunk. Ha! Newton a tree-hugger with apple pulp in his hair he thought he had it all figured out a universe of order of checks and balances cause and effect principals rules laws and order proven with sound mathematical equations. Well say hello to my Red Wings Isaac they're about to rise from rest and step on your first law of motion your law of inertia try not to land on your genius head when you fall off your high horse. Oh my sweet tattered Red Wings how I love you so dearly.

Back and forth back and forth in time in memory deceitful memory if only events all events and experiences could be recorded we could set to rewind and look back at what really happened but can we ever know what really happened? We view perceive feel experience through our own subjective prism or perhaps prison think Hiedegger relativity Rashomon Effect phenomenology. The preposterous unreliability of eye witness accounts of the same event the killer is the tall blond one with the spider web on his shaved head no it's clearly the short Black man with an earring and purple dreadlocks no you're both wrong the butler did it saw it with my own eyes. But memory nags the persistence of memory flaccid pliable like clocks watches melting on a surreal tree branch.

But we do our best with the memories we have and I suppose we must have faith ha ha faith flimsy faith unscientific faith in what we remember.

Faith. Is it a good thing, blind or otherwise? My memories are on the rise again. Memories of childhood. Of sickness and isolation. Of places where I did not want to be. Places like church.

Memories of Sunday Mass, where amidst the incoherence of Latin litany and the torment of interminable kneeling, I learned many things. Things I was not supposed to conjecture, let alone learn.

I learned that the Saints had once been priests, who were inspired by their passion for God and the sweet flesh of young boys. And I learned of the frustration of nuns, screaming in silence for Christ to slip from the cross and descend upon their loins- their neglected loins. If not him, then who?

And I learned of shame and guilt for transgressions never made. For sins never committed. And I learned of the power of fear. Fear of burning forever in Hell, and I learned of temptation, the temptation to turn away from guilt and shame and fear and turn to the Fallen One for refuge; to the Radiant One, the rebellious one of flies and insurrection.

And I remember, one day after mass, my boyhood curiosity getting the better of me, and venturing up to the balcony where I had never been, that mysterious place, fifteen feet closer to Heaven, the better to be snatched up in rapture. And I was alone, surrounded by pictures and statues of the saints. And then I was not alone. He appeared before me from out of the silent shadows, the big Irish priest imported from the Emerald Isle. Father Clarey, of the immense red face, reassigned to a new land, the American land, for reasons unspoken. These were different times. And I remember his slurred brogue, his breath reeking of wine, the blood of Jesus, as he came closer. And I ran- unscathed- or so I like to think.

Where am I now, my leathery friends? I remember and somewhat recently or at least not too distantly a woman a mystery woman a spectral but flesh and blood woman who would as if from smoke from a shrouded mist appear whenever I would step out the door. She wore sandals and sundresses always the same, dark hair set in a bun not slender not fat a bit pale something about her retro from another time from a cult perhaps. Uncanny. Whenever I would walk out the door (wearing guess what on my feet) she would walk out her door whenever I would arrive home from somewhere she would arrive home seconds before or seconds after. Synchronized strangers. I wonder can't help but wonder if she notices me if she has given me any thought if she finds a peculiar rhythm in our synchronicity does she find it odd does she find me odd? Those whispers those whispers again growing louder whispers from where from my father's grave you're timid oh gutless son of mine oh shame of my loins just walk up to her and introduce yourself howdy neighbor I live across the street but then the apparition woman from afar the woman the mystery woman would be a mystery no more.

Something just occurred to me. Do women wear Red Wings? Do they make Red Wings for women? I don't recall seeing any at the Red Wing store but it's been so long years millennia perhaps epochs since I've been in one it seems inappropriate incongruous women wearing Red Wings I know I know we're in an era of gender bending fluidity of sexual identity musical chairs of male and female pronouns colliding and careening masculine feminine common neuter he she them they straight crooked bi both neither. People don't know themselves what the hell they are anymore but still old fashioned boy that I am fresh off the oxymoron turnip truck jock straps for her by Calvin Klein and tampons for him a girl for you a boy for me oh how happy now we will be as long as women don't slip their dainty elegant feet into my precious Red Wings.

I'm beginning to wonder I must admit confess that this incessant fixation with my Red Wings my scuffed up beaten but not defeated Red Wings may not be entirely wholesome let's not even get into normal as if we can all agree on what constitutes normality who is truly normal we all have our quirks and fetishes our compulsions and obsessions we get away with most of them after all the great Central Authority that surveils us all is not entirely intolerant but back to normality such a wide swath of relativism I remember way back in the day a tattoo was a bold extreme statement a beacon of defiance a middle digit pointed at mores propriety acceptance societal niceties. Who bore them back in the day? Outlaw bikers ex-cons sailors who got drunk went on a bender got tattooed hating themselves in the morning Maggie inked within a heart not remembering who the hell Maggie is outsiders aberrant fringe people but whoa look at today how things change your dentist CPA personal trainer life counselor benign bagger at the checkout abound with tattoos on their arms legs torsos faces and not to mention a rising penchant for piercings brandings ritualistic self-mutilation we've come a long way baby today the unmarked pristine epidermis people are the freaks and wierdos so what is normal let me tell you about the most normal man who ever lived he hailed from Missouri and was a haberdasher he became president and with little reflection ordered atomic bombs dropped on Hiroshima then when everyone was in shock and could not respond he dropped another atomic bomb on Nagasaki hundreds of thousands of civilians died many in slow agony he was a common man named Harry just plain Harry he never lost a minute of sleep he was just like you and me well maybe you.

It's just so soothing to stare up at them every muscle every sinew every organ gland tooth nail node every abnormality deformity allergy every vestigial tail and remnant from the primordial ooze from which we wiggled from whence we came all quieted within a tranquil sea of lassitude. What if we all wore Red Wings? Would the world be a better place a kinder gentler place a warless crimeless rapeless place where everyone smiled at one another and kept smiling even when alone and we could sleep with our windows and doors unlocked and not worry about our hair and our waistlines and warts and wrinkles our sags and scars our savings and debt our health wealth weather our climate our immolating climate the rivers rising the icebergs melting the species dying the grapes withering on the vine the crops failing the sky is falling but keep your shoes on keep smiling smiling broader wider smile at the crows in the sky and the wolf at the door just keep smiling until your face splits in two until madness sets in sadly, sadly some things even Red Wings can't do.

Philosophy. Staring up at them, those Red Wings propped up on the couch yes they sooth and incite memory memories good and bad but they also inspire contemplation and the urge to wax philosophical.

Philosophy. Greek for love of wisdom. Here they are again those wondrous Greeks no not the ones today who seem like unlikely descendants but the ancient ones of antiquity come on you know who I mean Aristotle who was mentored by Plato who was a student of Socrates who invented the oft times annoying Socratic method endless argumentation not unlike Talmudic hair splitting but let's save the Jews for another time. Plato was an apt student and protégé of Socrates but knew when to keep his mouth shut but

Socrates who annoyed the entire city-state of Athens kept on yakkin' until they simply couldn't take it anymore and you know what came next he didn't drink the Kool-Aid but quaffed the hemlock and it was good bye Mr. Chips.

But my Red Wings do draw out the philosophy in me and let's face it to endure the indignities of life the endless effronteries of experience one must be philosophical but to which philosophy should one ascribe? The list is long there's Stoicism Aristotelianism Episcopalianism oops veering into religion now though there is some overlap and isn't Buddhism more of a philosophy than a religion and Jainism more of a religion than a philosophy so many to choose from something for everyone Nihilism Absurdism Cynicism Idealism and Skepticism ha that one challenges the veracity the validity of all the others and then there's Quietism the perfect philosophy for the hung over.

Absurdism. Now there's a philosophy. It posits there is no inherent meaning zero nada zilch and so the individual must forge meaning within the meaninglessness. Probably not the best choice for the unimaginative but ah the possibilities to heroically take on a meaningless chaotic universe a wasteland without a map an endless sea without a sextant or for that matter dead reckoning or the North Star don't hope for a rescue ship or a bright beckoning beacon a lighthouse with a myopic narcoleptic keeper is more likely or a search party of blind babbling fools it's all you baby you're a big boy now it's all you as you venture into the void teetering on a tightrope without a net and alone.

But-the power. The intoxicating power. You want justice in the world the cruel cold world then put it there you want a moral creed a personal code of honor draw one up who's to stop you a cop a priest a prune sucking librarian whose only function in life is to hiss **shhhh!** Well your beliefs principles values are as good, no, make that better than theirs because they do what the law, the Good Book, Robert's Rules Of Order, Miss Prudence's Book Of Etiquette tell them to do. How do they know the Bible tells them so like baaing sheep docile obedient dumb not aware that the pleasant walk through the pasture is in fact a death march off to slaughter. It's all you baby. No one at your back no posse compatriots comrades reinforcements cavalry it's all you baby, alone, all alone. Now full speed ahead.

Did I mention that with the purchase of each pair of Red Wings comes a lifetime supply of free laces? I'm pretty sure I did but it bears repeating that's quite a perk considering the longevity durability and tenacity of these magnificent shoes. And what a propitious time to bring this up for as I stare up at my magnificent shoes I notice the one on the right has a lace frayed nearly to the breaking point and would probably snap with one hardy tug. People usually snap shoelaces when they're late for important appointments but that's of little concern to me because I never go anywhere. There's a good and bad side to everything. Years back there was a serial murderer called The Freeway Killer no not because he murdered freeways which would wreak havoc with peoples' daily commutes no he was called that because he would pick up hitchhikers and drug them and hogtie them with their own shoelaces before torturing and killing them. Well if he tried that on me one sharp yank and I would be free and escape or who knows even better get the upper hand and hogtie him with <u>his</u> own shoelaces then call the police and the news media and bask in the spotlight of heroic notoriety and forever be known as the guy who captured The Freeway Killer I'm the man you bet I am I'm the Red Wing Man.

I'm drifting drifting back in memory once again and I think I'm about seven and my parents were debating about whether or not I should be allowed to stay up late and see a scary movie. My mother was concerned that at my tender age the potential trauma might warp my mind ha little did she know the cornucopia of trauma the prolonged Mother Lode of traumas yet to come but she was overruled by my father. Who knows, he may have relished the thought of trauma forever afflicting the fragile innocent psyche of his only begotten son. And thus I was allowed to stay up late and watch the original 1933 version of King Kong.

I was fascinated. Mesmerized and captivated. The movie so dark, nocturnal and dream-like and years later I would discover that this film was embraced by Andre Breton and the French Surrealists. But I was confused, that innocent young psyche of mine never having been exposed to ambiguity, and wasn't Kong, the fifty-two foot tall Magnificent Ape and Eighth Wonder Of The World, supposed to be the villain what with abducting poor diminutive Fay Wray? God only knows what he intended to do with her (my innocent young psyche was not sufficiently developed to conjecture the possibilities, although Andre Breton and his pals probably could, what with them being French and all), but I was on Kong's side from the get go and it felt strange. Weren't the good guys cops vs. robbers cowboys vs. Indians (oops indigenous people) white hats versus black hats wasn't it supposed to be clear and simple self-evident a priori yin and yang? If Kong wasn't the bad guy then who was? He didn't go to The Big Apple of his own volition, no they gassed him unconscious and abducted him. He was a hostage and boy if there was ever anyone immune to the Stockholm Syndrome it was Kong- King Fucking Kong! Shackled, debased, humiliated, a giant Broadway attraction, a gargantuan vaudeville performer, growling, pulling on his chains inspiring awe and fear in the heartless gown and tuxedoed audience. Atta boy, give the people their money's worth, and if they're not shitting their pants yet, well in just a few moments there will be an excremental extravaganza. Then, like self-destructive idiots, they cart out Fay Wray on stage with her rescuer beau, a guy named Jack and Kong's hated rival. And the press, the drooling paparazzi, begin snapping pictures- flash bulbs flaring, agitating the big fellow, and a voice screams out, "Stop-stop, he thinks you're hurting the girl!" and with a mighty tug he is unchained, liberated, pissed off to high heaven running amok, killing and crushing hapless bystanders, derailing subway trains- looking- searching desperately for her. Fay Wray where did they hide her? There! He finds her in a hotel room as he climbs building after building, and reaching through the window he snatches her from the insipid Jack. And my innocent young psyche grapples with what is transpiring, perplexed and bewildered, not the least of reasons being I sensed Fay actually preferred Kong over Jack, because he was pure and uncorrupted. Then, my epiphany. I'm with you Kong, I'm with you, wreak havoc on the bastards, grab Fay Wray, climb up the newly constructed Empire State Building, that phallic concrete and steel icon of industrial civilization. No, no, here come the planes yes, knock them out of the sky with your massive fist, but the cowards have you outnumbered blasting you with machine guns death by a thousand cuts and you fall, fall to the street below, dead. And as your body is surrounded by gawking onlookers, a cop tells Kong's captor, "Well, it looks like the planes got him." And he replies with a rueful smile, "No- twas beauty killed the beast." Bullshit. You killed him, you exploitive bastard, and before the closing credits I'm even more convinced and no longer ambivalent. I knew then I was one of you and not one of them, and as far as I'm concerned you should have laid waste to New York, then moved onto Jersey.

I know, I don't get sufficient exercise, lying on my back and staring at my Red Wings. It's a miracle I don't have bed sores, or, more accurately, couch sores. I've had them before, but that was a lifetime ago in a place where no one cared (not that anyone cares here and now, oh poor pitiful weepy me.) Bedsores. Patient neglect. A common reason today for medical malpractice litigation. No one cared. And I survived. And now I'm no longer an ill frightened child. If I wanted to rise from the couch now I have the power. But do I have the will and desire?

Sometimes I wonder if they think we're all a bunch of fools. Pea brains, mutton-heads, dimwits, dull, dumb, dullards, witless brainless bubbleheads. You know. They. The proverbial They as in central authority infallible experts. We know what's best for you. What's best for us is best for you. What's best for us is turning a buck off you gullible born yesterday there's one born every minute you. Example: Advertising. I wonder, surmise, posit, postulate that the vast majority and I mean vast as in the vast ocean, sky, wasteland vast of goods, products, services pitched at us are not only not what they're cracked up to be but are useless at best and deadly at worst. The drugs they literally try to cram down our throats for vague, arcane, perhaps non-existent maladies, for killer conditions, why people are dropping like flies from the dreaded restless leg syndrome, the debilitating gerd, the heartbreaking psoriasis, those horrific facial tics that are a side effect of our anti-psychotic medications, and the endless array of anti-depressants, so many different kinds, flavors, like Baskin Robbins for our heads. As if being depressed in the world we live in isn't a natural state of being- it's universal, or at least should be. It's the happy ones who should be medicated so they can recognize reality and be miserable like the rest of us. The conditions, diseases, syndromes seem to come and go with changing fashion or maybe they've milked us dry and new ailments must be introduced to replace the obsolete. Remember Carpel Tunnel Syndrome? Hypoglycemia? Chronic Fatigue Syndrome? Where did they go or maybe they were never really here. Save your money revel in your misery your nerve endings need the exercise, clap your hands, stomp your feet rub your wrists make them red is that a rash or stigmata? Forgive the bastards for they know not what they do or crucify them- because they know exactly what they're doing.

I wonder when people first started wearing shoes? Not shoes per say but protective footwear. The Ice Age? People must have had unbelievably tough feet pre-footwear. It's tough enough walking barefoot on pavement or asphalt like in August when the heat is so intense you could smell the asphalt, and when you realize you should be wearing shoes or sandals but it's too late and you begin a ridiculous looking hop skip and you want to turn back but you realize you are half way to your destination so suck it in partner grin and bear it show some grit some moxey some manhood, offensive as that might be, separate yourself from the boys listen to your soles sizzle your heels holler someday when you write your memoirs make reference to the experience if only in your footnotes.

All right. Memories again. The memories weave in and out like glimpses of the moon on a cloudy night. How old was I? Not that young and not that old. Let me tell you about the addiction. Let me tell you about cocaine.

I had a job. Blue collar, warehouse, moving things around with a pallet jack and forklift. Oh what an odd milieu for someone of my sensibilities, but such are circumstances. Friday nights. I would meet with a small

group of co-workers after work for drinks during
"happy hour." Ha- what an absurd term. Happy hour?
What's so happy about it? There are people who
commit suicide after happy hour, or, inebriated to the
point of semi-consciousness, wreak unspeakable roadway carnage en-route going home. Oh listen to me such
a sourpuss it's amazing my co-workers included me in
their TGIF imbibements. We talk. We talk about drugs.
Everyone at the table was a cocaine user and were
probably high as they spoke of the bliss and euphoria of
"The Snow," "The Blow," "The White Lady," and I
chimed that although I had tried many drugs oh
innocent me I had never tried cocaine. A brief moment
of quiet. One of the group, a slender fellow, a charming
chap named Ramon who we all knew had done time,
smiled a funny little smile, and when we met the
following Friday night I rose from the table to use the
rest room where people never rest it should more
properly be called the waste room because people in
fact go there to eliminate waste or get wasted or both.
How odd it seemed that I was followed at my heels by
Ramon and as soon as the door closed Ramon, who was
rather androgynous in appearance, shoved me into a
stall and oh no I had heard of such things- fight or
flight, hand to hand combat time, self-defense, preserve
my manly dignity, be what it is. Who knows what
perverse practices Ramon had learned in jail but no- he
had other ideas. In a flash he whipped out a small vile
of white powder scooped up a bit with a ridiculously

small spoon and brought it to my nostrils. I sniffed a deep sniff then he instructed me, wise mentor that he was, to rub the small bit of remaining powder in the spoon over my gums then we walked back to the bar and joined the others. For a moment there was nothing-like what's the big deal another anticlimactic experience among countless ones then it hit. A slow rainbow of sensations amped up like with speed but blended with a calm euphoria and an odd sense of confidence and women in our group or within the bar women who had seemed conspicuously ordinary now had become Goddesses, glowing beacons of eroticism and the lights and colors in the bar quivered with undulating excitement fascination and oh White Lady where have you been all my life please allow me to kiss your hand and save the last dance for me.

Addiction. Cocaine is not physically addictive but neither are blood red sunsets and women with raven hair and green eyes. Addiction is not dose dependent. If only one line of cocaine a year is sniffed you're addicted if that one line is all you think about. Obsessed craving- duplication of that first experience. They say the best line you'll ever sniff is that first one. Oh Ramon was a clever dealer. That first line and the first few grams I bought from him were pure and uncut. Then, after the hook is in, the quality drops and gets adulterated. Stepped on. Ramon confessed he cut his product with baby laxative, confident the revelation would not deter me from being a repeat customer. I couldn't believe this was happening to me. I never got this way with drink or other drugs, being disciplined and not getting in over my head. The seductive power of the White Lady the excitement the anticipation brewing days before the score, that anticipation being part of the high. The clandestine drive home after the score; the added thrill of risk if busted. Back in the day even with only a few grams there would be consequences, and consequences are rarely good.

And it went on for years. In hindsight it was fortunate my sources came and went and long periods often elapsed before I would connect with a new source, a new dealer, and during those years I went to places where I never should have gone and associated with people I never should have known. The White Lady, seductive like sweet dreams from which you never want to awake, like The Land Of The Lotus Eaters, like the hypnotic songs of the Sirens, like Death teasing and cajoling. Principles loosen, morals sag, lies are told, stupid risks taken. Finally, the day of reckoning. I bought three grams, not cut with baby laxative but with meth speed kills my heart pounding as if trying to kick out of my chest had I known I never would have done line after line why should I have known deception is part of the trade finally, when Death, decked out like The White Lady stuck her tongue in my ear and whispered, so soft and sweetly, "I

am the love of your life- come- come home with me,"
finally I did it, The White Lady flushed down the toilet,
down, down into the sewer, down all the way to Hell.

I'm back, back in the saddle again, back where a
shoe is a friend I stare upward, there they are the old
reliables and such an anomaly why don't I cramp or get
gangrene from lack of circulation well the rules of
medicine of physiology aren't infallible and rules were
made to be broken just like records and hearts. What
now? I need something different. A change of pace.
Step right up, folks.

I see. I see a man on a tightrope above a ballerina
doing pirouettes atop an elephant. Off to the side a
strongman in a leopard skin bathing suit lifts an
immense barbell. He is flanked by two slender men
with handlebar moustaches, identical twins, one thrusts
a fiery torch down his throat as another pounds a nail
into his head. A frenzy of activity a three ring circus
horses doing tricks atop the shoulders of trapeze artists
and a spider monkey dressed up as a ringmaster all
under the Big Top ah yes high art for the masses.

Then: a thundering drum roll. The flurry of activity
is halted. Silence. Someone in the audience drops a pin.
Everyone hears it for such is the profundity of the
silence the quiet of stone cold deafness, of the aftermath
of annihilation, the quiet of graveyards after visiting

hours, the quiet of saints, gaping mouthed saints with their tongues torn off, the quiet of sound itself after it has been murdered, smothered with a pillow by a mute assassin.

The silence is broken. The spider monkey ringmaster roars like a lion. "Ladies and gentlemen, I proudly present to you the main attraction, the reason- the true reason you are here tonight! Don't deny it the truth shall set you free! You would kill to experience what you are about to see and not just once or twice ladies and gentlemen, oh no you would launch into a frenzy of obsessive compulsive serial homicide to see and savor the unbelievable, the indefatigably captivating, **Consuela The Confounding Contortionist!!**

Cannons are fired and clowns are jettisoned from the smoking barrels there is a cloud of smoke billowing to the sound of trumpets and from the smoky billows she appears. There is hysteria in the audience, a rapture of delirium, then silence again. Rapt silence.

She is lovely and lithe as she smiles, the smile of innocence and of guile her blond hair cropped short she looks like a pixie and moves like a sprite then, with a bow and a curtsy she falls to the ground prone, still, immobile.

She is clad in an odd snakeskin leotard so tight it looks like her own skin and perhaps it is then the act commences. She begins to slither on her belly undulating like a real serpent. With a hiss her tongue darts out wiggling from her mouth and grows in length until it is stretched a hundred feet from her mouth a loud collective murmur of oohs and ahs erupts from the rapt audience then her tongue whips backward and wraps around her left leg and pulls until her leg is vertical ninety degrees and her tongue keeps pulling until Consuela begins to rise hoisted upward by her own tongue how how can this be is this illusion delusion or perhaps sorcery she keeps rising until she has reached the top of the tent and the audience oohs and ahs then Consuela's tongue wraps around her other leg and her arms and her legs are stretched, drawn away from her body, stretched longer and longer and now stuck on the tent's ceiling she appears to be a four pointed star then her body becomes florescent glowing like a true star and the audience goes ooh and ah then- a scream. Consuela screams and falls from the lofty height of the tent top plummeting inexorably and going splat on the circus floor and the audience applauds wildly ah well it was good while it lasted and now what will the next act be? But wait. Consuela is not through yet. Her broken body and shattered limbs begin moving, undulating again within the snakeskin leotard then her left leg detaches from her body and then the right as both arms break away from her torso and they all begin to morph suddenly her limbs have turned into real snakes vipers with huge mouths gaping like caverns fangs long sharp like scythes sharpened and bathed in venom then the spider monkey ring master summons two assistants who lift Consuela's head and torso and place her on a jewel studded throne, "Yes, yes my children, grow and be strong" she shouts to the snakes and they expand, each the size of a whale. "Yes, yes my darling babies, you must eat to be strong!"and the serpents set upon the audience oohs and ahs becoming blood curdling screams and there beneath the big top one and all are swallowed by the giant serpents and oh my what a night to remember!

An interesting thought has come to me. It has occurred out of the blue out of left field a notion of spontaneous origin or perhaps transmitted to my psyche via satellite from an ancient race of extraterrestrials billions of light years away they observe us have always observed us and when bored they provoke thoughts into our minds which on our own would never have germinated. Here's the thought: What if, pure conjecture, but what if I had worn Red Wings as a child? Would the entire saga of my life spiraled into other directions perhaps, no, almost certainly, happier healthier superior directions? I'm staring up at them now those scuffed ruggedly handsome protectors of my feet and not to mention sanity fragile and tenuous as it might be. Here's the rub. How long ago was it when I was a child? I have memories of childhood and often remember my age within those memories but I'm not entirely sure how long ago I was of a given age I remember the ages attached to various traumas at five ten eleven fifteen but how long ago was that, which places me in the awkward embarrassing position or so it would seem of not knowing how old I am now or for that matter even what year it is now. This is mortifying as you can well imagine. Ah. Flashes of childhood memories I'm not sick in a hospital bed no I'm outdoors playing a game now look down what do I see tennis shoes just as I suspected now it's conjecture time: What if I looked down and saw *Red Wings For Boys* who knows what might have been?

There have been times when I drift off to sleep but for moments only as I stare at the marvelous fabulous (uh oh tangent alert- I've heard some say pejoratively that only gay men use the adjectives marvelous and fabulous to which I respond who gives a flying fuck except pea brained evangelical preachers spewing their homophobic hatred as they are busted in public bathroom stalls brains sizzling on crystal meth hypocritically ignoring the awkwardness of male hustlers' shafts stuck like barnacles to their backsides "Oh I can explain this officer, just give me a few days conferring with my attorney") shoes propped up on the couch as they are wont to be. On two nights in succession I experienced what I would describe as mini-semi-dreams during my drift offs that were nearly identical. Here goes: In my dream I am lying on my couch as I am in actuality and I seemingly wake up rise and walk into the kitchen. It all seems so real then I notice the changes subtle at first but soon becoming insidious. I look around it is all so normal then, when I attempt to return to the couch, a wall in the kitchen has grown wider and the opening so narrow I can barely squeeze through back to the living room. I look about. Something else has changed. The clutter. All of the clutter on the kitchen counters, my desk and my table has been removed. A moment of rejoice! Some kind, caring benefactor (or more probably benefactress as women are more inclined to neatness and boy now I'm really off into sexist stereotyping to say nothing of tangential rambling!) has snuck into my home unawares and tidied things up for me but whoa. My important papers writing projects meaningful miscellaneous keepsakes and written reminders have been discarded along with the clutter. A wave of panic a sense of violation set in, the baby thrown out with the bathwater a brutish benefactor (or benefactress) with no ability to discern or differentiate that which should be discarded from that which is legitimately precious slash and burn what the hell do my feelings or preferences have to do with anything and I wonder. I wonder if my sisters have broken and entered, trespassed to impose their will their ill-will their synchronized malevolent will upon my life just like old times. It all seems so real too real. I look at my TV screen the TV. is not on but somehow images and forms appear on the screen frightening bizarre images faces twisted contorted masks like evil witchdoctor masks and shrunken heads the look of horror frozen on the faces freeze dried the look of death suddenly realized. I'm starting to get what is happening, why this is a dream and now I must will myself awake I jump up and down and bite my thumb but there is no pain just numbness this dream does not want me to leave then from out of the shadows a dark figure appears wearing a black hat face hidden in darkness "Who are you!" I scream. "You know who I am," the figure replies. Now the fear rises bubbles up from a pit inside me wake up wake up the dark figure moves closer is it him The Grim Reaper or worse- my father? Then I'm back lying on the couch and staring at the pictures on the wall I'm getting there but not yet there's a split in the vision of my right eye I'm awakening the pictures appear normal familiar but through my left eye the pictures are twisted distorted and the struggle the struggle begins there is a war a tug of war if I concentrate on the pictures on my right I will wake up I'm almost there - but my gaze is being drawn to my left and if my will breaks and the left takes me the dream has won and I will be pulled into madness or death from which there is no awakening then – I'm back! Wide awake and on my back sweet Red Wings I've never been so glad to see you don't change don't ever change.

Memories again drawn back in time the bleak memories the dark ones the ones that remind us how brutal life can be they too can bully dominate elbow the good memories away the good memories hopelessly outnumbered fighting the good fight the dark fight.

I'm recuperating a few weeks out of the hospital my first tour of duty in the hospital so I must be ten. Hot. Hot summer day. I'm in a car without air conditioning. The whole family five of us stuck inside a car I'm in back with my two sisters, my mother in front with my father who's in the driver's seat. We're driving through the desert the endless desert as other cars whiz by my father does not believe in driving fast. I look at my father. He's chewing gum the muscles in his neck the back of his neck move and contract with each chew. We're driving home from a brief vacation a desert vacation the Grand Canyon, the Petrified Forest and Las Vegas. As we would stop for gas and soft drinks I discovered in the vending machines a large variety of soft drinks that were unfamiliar to me. Brands and names and flavors, a multitude of designs and colors, endless variety, and people would open their soft drink bottles with an opener attached to the vending machine and the bottle caps would fall into a receptacle below. And thus was the beginning of my bottle cap collection.

It was exciting, my bottle cap collection. With each stop I would discover new brands and color schemes not seen on the prior stops. For the first time on the trip I felt some joy and satisfaction and eventually I had a bag filled with my precious bottle cap treasure and as we drove through the desert I made the enormous mistake of expressing rhapsodically my happiness and the older of the two sisters, harpy number one, would have none of it and with the voice of a bitch hag she screamed, "I'm tired of hearing about these stupid bottle caps!" and she grabbed the bag from my hands and threw it out the window. Oh such joy in that car! The younger sister, harpy number two, the eyeball gouging sister, was near orgasmic with glee and dear old dad reveled in his own ecstasy, there was that sound he would make when I was tormented, a strange high pitched sound, a cross between a giggle and a squeal and for a moment I thought the old boy would pull over, get out of the car and jack off on the side of the road. And I must give credit where credit is due. My mother intervened and we drove back and I retrieved my precious bag of bottle caps but wait, don't go away, the best is yet to come.

Like many a young lad I was fascinated by monsters and the bizarre by strange creatures and anything or anyone misshapen, mutilated, mutated, all anomalies and aberrant oddities- in general, all that was weird. And as we drove back home through the endless desert inside the slow moving four wheeled torture chamber a sign appeared on the roadside. **See The**

Unbelievable Thing! Ten Miles Ahead. Shaking with
anticipation, I blurted, "Can we stop and see it!" And
my father, completely out of character, seemed to
actually share my excited enthusiasm and wondrous
anticipation and replied, "You bet- I'm dying to see
what this thing is- I can hardly wait!" And as we drove
through the arid wasteland past the endless yuccas
another sign appeared. **The Incredible Indescribable
Thing! Seven Miles Ahead.** As we drove onward,
closer, with my excitement growing and my father's
flushed beaming face reflected in the rear view mirror, I
mused, finally, my father, my dad, connecting with his
only begotten son with a shared fascination, then
another sign. **You Won't Believe Your Eyes- The
Eighth Wonder Of The World! Two Miles Ahead.**
Then another sign as we crept across the desert the
cruel tragic desert it was the last sign. **The Strangest
Most Disturbing Sight You'll Ever See- Be
Prepared! Next Turn-Off.** And there it was. A narrow
dirt road with arrows pointing toward the entrance, and
my father, <u>more</u> excited than I, slowed to a crawl and
began to turn, then, straightened the car and slammed
on the accelerator and there was that glass shattering
giggle squeal of sheer sadistic glee bellowing from his
mouth and my dear sisters, screaming like banshees
being rutted by demons and my mother, my poor
imperfect mother who had some love and empathy for
her son hung her head in her hands, with weakness and
with shame and oh how my tears flowed and one day,

years later, my father would die of cancer. Regrets. We all have them, though not all of us, like my father have remorse. Two of my regrets: That I never told him that I would have been better off with no father at all, and I regret more that when he died, it wasn't with my hands around his neck.

I'm refocused now the lucidity of trauma absurd ancient trauma begins to fade, begins to fog and when things clear what a sight for sore eyes there they are the stalwart ones the intractable ones noble and true I present to you ladies and gentlemen my beloved Red Wings. I stare. Rapt. Ideas and questions ferment. The big questions. I ponder.

Are we Good or are we Evil? Such a child-like question, black and white, in a nutshell, either or, no consideration of nuance, gradation, range scale or continuum. What, for that matter, is Good and Evil? Are they relative, subjective, subject to change in an eternal state of flux, influenced by evolving mores fashions flavors of the month flavors of the millennia ebbs and flows fluctuations of the stock market of the Dow of the Tao the length of skirts and the shortness of breath? No. More likely Good and Evil are pliable, clay in the potter's hands, bendable, pliant to the smithy's hammer retooled revised reinvented by whatever authority rules the roost at whatever given time. Absolute. Absolute definitions of Good and Evil? Says who? You have to believe someone, usually God. What God? Who's God? Whatever God you were told of indoctrinated with as a child. So many competing Gods the God of Allah of Abraham of the angel named Moroni (ah- an Italian God?) the Yahwey God **The One True God** everyone they all think the other is the false God the cult God who to believe what would happen if you believed in none perhaps you are a searcher blind wandering with a white cane better go down the right path or you might stumble and fall into the abyss. But, having said all that, could there be a consensus a solidarity perhaps universality yes that's asking a lot but the Golden Rule is valid independent of a God I don't want to be whacked over the head with a two by four so I won't whack someone else with one. Are empathy and compassion dependent upon the grace of God, or are they inherent, hardwired into people who feel the pain of others and want to mitigate suffering? I would posit those people just described are good and those people who are devoid of empathy and want to inflict suffering are evil. Building an orphanage is good; burning one to the ground is evil, especially after the innocent orphans have been tucked in, probably after saying their prayers, thus compounding their suffering-good God do you need a hearing aid!? But here's the rub the fly in the ointment the elephant in the room: In a material world a universe of matter and energy and nothing else can good and evil be palpable measurable observable under the microscope detectable through the telescope in the world of science good and evil have no atomic code no gnome no fossil record therefore they are metaphysical why even waste our time so say the scientists why bother we have better things to do leave these questions to the fools and philosophers go away and debate among yourselves how many angels can stand on the head of a pin? A question. A provocative question. Can there be good without evil or evil without good? Can there be a yin without yang a north without south tall without short rich without poor? But. But what if there is no balance polarity no eternal law of opposites darkness without light Hell without Heaven? And so I have descended into the sinkhole the pit the abyss of pessimism of doubt of cynicism. I believe in Hell but am skeptical of Heaven. I have seen evil a malignant mist a halo of darkness I have seen it etched on faces a virus moving through assemblies becoming crowds then the halos appear one for everyone radiating darkness the crowd shifts becomes a mob I have seen the leer of evil the smug jubilation of the mob the wide mouths obscene gaping holes grinning with glee at the carnival at the warm Summer night's picnic- smile for the camera try not to drool as Black men hang from the trees, swaying in the Summer breeze.

It's funny. A peculiarity. I'm staring up at the good ole' Red Wings propped up on the couch which may belong to them by now they've been up there so long perhaps they've taken ownership through adverse possession but how can title to a couch be transferred there's no metes and bounds no legal description nor unpaid property tax? But that's not the peculiarity. It seems I've been staring at them for an eternity and it's peculiar that my feet never itch. I would think an occasional foot itch would be universal regardless of the merits of the particular shoes and Red Wings are indeed meritorious but still nary a single foot itch? What does that mean? Are they so impregnable impervious to outside stimuli that my feet are shielded from the indignities the effronteries the slings and arrows of outrageous fleas tics mites mosquitoes to say nothing of the insidious fungi mange crud rashes scratches blisters bunions corns callouses and all the other endless array of itch producing entities novelties oddities and whatever else is drawn to the human foot like moths to the flame. My feet simply do not itch when I have my Red Wings on which means they never itch period because my Red Wings are never off. So stick that in your pipe and smoke it.

Friendships. Some people have many some people have none. A friend in need is a friend indeed. Who comes up with these folkisms, anyway? They annoy me they stick in my craw rub me the wrong way and, God help me, get my goat. Ye gads! I said it! Ha! Now I'm doing it, spewing stupid folkisms to express my distaste for stupid folkisms. It's hard to avoid for such is our lexicon, riddled with buffoonish aphorisms and crusty old folk sayings. They're tough to avoid even for snobs like myself like a dog shaking fleas see what I mean maybe I should stop fighting it go with the flow completely acquiesce slip a corncob pipe in my mouth put on a pair of bib overalls a straw hat jump on the Grand Ole' Opry stage ah shucks smack a spoon against my thigh and sing, "Jimmy Crack Corn, And I Don't Care" listen to the roar of the crowd they love me which brings me back to friendship.

Friendship. Precarious. Whose side are you really on? Betrayal. The bright side of friendlessness is you'll never be betrayed or disappointed. You'll never have people dropping in on you unexpectedly and it's always at the worst possible time your place is a mess you are a mess your pet cat just died possibly at your own hands you're in the middle of a fevered masturbation session you were picking your nose and your finger is stuck. And their attitude. "I just happened to be in the neighborhood and thought I'd just stop by!" As if boy this is your lucky day the arrogance the blinding ray of narcissism as they smile so pleased with themselves by the special treat they've provided you the privilege of their presence the sense of joy and gratitude you undoubtedly feel for their filling the lonely gap in your miserable life. And of course you are expected to express your gratefulness with a meal a drink a glass of cognac a line of cocaine a back rub and the pink slip to your car. Wouldn't it be nice refreshing perhaps even transformationally cathartic to draw a bead on their smug grinning faces and punch them in the mouth look them in the eye and tell them to get the fuck out and never come back?

All right. Maybe this is just sour grapes because I have so few friends why I could count them on the fingers of one hand actually on the finger of one hand and which finger you ask why the middle one that got lopped off in an industrial accident or maybe bitten off by a hungry dog I was trying to feed and yes no good deed will go unpunished.

Speak to me Red Wings as I so look up to you which is both a choice and an inevitability as I now seem to be an implant on the couch and the only way I can look is up. Take me back lift the fog of memory excise the cataracts clouding my past.

I remember. As far back as I can remember I was a loner. Different in some essential ways from the other boys who roamed around in groups gangs and packs. Strength in numbers allowing behaviors that would be condemned and prohibited if done individually. I think of Carol hapless innocent Carol and the hurt and humiliation she endured at the hands of the bullies. A question arises: Nature versus nurture. Was I born a loner, or did I decide to become one as a retreat a recoil from the bullies in my life the countless bullies the familial bullies at home the bullies in the playground in the neighborhood in the classroom in the hospital the students and teachers and doctors and nurses who were bullies. Such a strong argument for nurture oh such a grotesque oxymoron as if bullying is a nurturing behavior.

Now for the nature argument. Perhaps I was born a loner. My solitary nature forged within the womb probably causing excruciating cramps for my mother. A need a desire to be if not lonely but simply alone happier when kept to myself hardwired etched in the gnome in the code in the grand biological scheme of things which ironically could make one a target of the bullies let's **get** him he's outnumbered he's always by himself what a weirdo *the other* why even the other packs tribes don't seem to want him a pariah an outcast in which case a double whammy a loner by nature exacerbated by nurture. But I always felt this need to be set apart from the others, especially after I discovered comic books.

Comic books of a certain genre became a kind of refuge for me a portal into another world a better more fascinating world a world that featured monsters but not like the real monsters of real life that could and would hurt and humiliate me. The horror and fantasy comics became my friends and salvation and there were many with titles like *Journey Into Mystery*, *Tales Of Suspense*, *Tales of Astonishment*, *Tales to Astound* and perhaps anticlimactically, *Strange Tales*. They were all published by the same company and featured the same writers and artists. Oh such excitement there were three small mom and pop grocery stores within walking distance that all sold comics and I would go to all of them once a month with allowance in hand and buy a stack then sneak into a secret hiding place a nook behind the garage or an ivy covered niche behind a looming avocado tree alone with my treasured comics immune at least for a while horror comics a shield against the true horrors of cruel people in a cruel world.

It didn't matter. It didn't matter that the stories were all variations on a theme and that the monsters all resembled one another the redundant covers: a horrific gargantuan creature hovering over a group of terrified people the monster bellowing lines something like, "Flee mortals- flee before the awesome might of Gomdulla!" The stories had few preliminaries an unspeakable monster hell bent on world domination or worse, annihilation, our armies impotent against them our scientists feeble minded in concocting a defense then in the end with humanity teetering on the brink of destruction trembling before the massive face of an outrageous creature that often looked like a cross between a gorilla and a gila monster the monster would be inexplicably thwarted meet his doom come crashing down by something infinitely dumb stupidly hokey i.e. the sound from little Bobby Dawkin's bike when he rode it with playing cards clothes pinned to the spokes made the hideous beast's head explode, or he would melt into a gooey slime from the delicious aroma of Mrs. Baker's cherry pie cooling on the window sill because on his planet cherry pie fumes are equivalent to mustard gas. The redundancy the revolving array of monsters and unlikely heroes and villains evil people betraying their own specie in exchange for immortality or infinite wealth monsters from outer space from beneath the ground from other dimensions from scientific experiments gone insanely awry from curses unleashed by violating the religions of obscure native tribes monsters from the graveyard from below the sea and yes, monsters from the ID from Freud's darkest theories life is unsafe one false move they're everywhere behind the door beneath the bed inside the barn beneath the tarn up the flagpole down the hatch but ironically for the boy isolated and alone safe for at least a little while within his inner sanctum hideout those magnificent monsters were friends. They too were different. Outcasts, pariahs, the frightened mortals cowering before them would turn into a vicious mob if they got the upper hand they would be destroyed decimated sometimes out of self-defense but other times simply because they were different justification enough simply because they were different.

I feel. I feel as if I am awakening from a trance emerging from a fog whiffing the smelling salts focus returns and the first thing I see well guess if they could speak they would say, "Welcome back, old friend," that's just the kind of shoes they are those dog gone Red Wings.

And now what? And now where? What and where will my memories take me next?

How long ago? How old was I? I'm not sure probably an adult older than a child. I hear music. There is a man playing an accordion. There is a sign next to him. *Father of six, fallen on hard times*. His wife and children sit behind him on a bench as he plays the sweet sad beautiful music memories within memories where have I heard this wonderful music before? It sounds French though I'm not sure why I hear it that way. Mediterranean perhaps? Where have I heard this music-have I heard it? Soulful wistful music played on an instrument I ordinarily don't care for until now. There is money in his open accordion case. I add five dollars and tell him his music is beautiful and evocative. I tell him that it reminds me of Sicily and that I am Sicilian. He asks how long I've been in this country. "Forever," I reply. There is an awkward moment, for his music is not evoking my memories, but my mother's memories, perhaps somehow more vivid for me than they ever were for her.

My mother was born in Sicily. When she was two
her mother died in the great pandemic of 1918. The
war to end all wars, the most absurdly monikered war if
not the most brutal, had just ended. You'd think
humanity deserved a breather, a brief respite, some
down time in order to regroup rethink recuperate
reconsider the efficacy of war but no. Through the
grace of God or randomness a one two punch first war
then pestilence can famine be far behind and what was
the fourth horse called that horse of a different color a
straggler late for The Apocalypse oh well three are
enough Mankind's on the ropes a fourth horse would be
superfluous gilding the lily of horror and despair and
there I go again with my tangential rambling I guess I
just can't help myself.

My mother came across the deep blue sea with her
four siblings. She was the youngest just as I was her
youngest. Their father came to the New Land first as
was the custom to save money before sending for his
children. They came in steerage on board the great ship
the *Giuseppe Verdi,* bidding adieu to the warm
Mediterranean climes. It was a cold dreary December
when they arrived. First there was the cattle count of
the huddled masses on Ellis Island then onward to cold
upstate New York to the new world to the new life. Oh
poor motherless child. Mother there were reasons for

your imperfections and I loved you dearly and you bequeathed your memories to me.

Oh my dear and loyal Red Wings I wonder as I stare up at you are you staring back at me? If so, what do you see? A pitiful creature bound to his couch with ropes of lethargy with chains of defeatism pressed by the weight of hopelessness will and spirit cracked and ready to crumble? I hope you see more if you can see at all.

Where are you taking me now, oh Red Wings? Not down memory lane but down a different path. A conjectural path. A path that leads to another one of the big questions. One of the big human condition questions. Here it is: Why did we evolve with such an immense capacity for suffering?

Pain, immediate pain, has purpose. When we early Hominids learned to make fire pain was a signal that we should not try to grasp the beautiful undulating flames look at those flames those mesmerizing seductive colors blue orange yellow so tempting to touch fluid ghostly dancers shimmying beckoning, "Come near", the flames whisper, "I will keep you warm come closer big boy reach out -oh how dare you!" You can look but you better not touch oh those teasing flirting flames one touch and there is agony as well there should be for without pain simple Hominids that we are we would gawk stupidly as our hand burned and bubbled into a useless charred mass dangling from the wrist. Yes, we need that kind of reflexive rapid fire pain or we would self-destruct from the endless array of insults to the flesh and pain is a teacher informing us of our frailties, vulnerabilities and limitations.

But suffering. The pain that lingers after we pull away from the fire the chronic pain that attaches to us like a leach long after we have removed ourselves from dangerous injurious external stimuli. And then there is the endless spectrum of emotional and psychological suffering the suffering of loss of heartbreak of unrequited love of watching those we love die and leave and for those of us with heightened sensitivity and compassion the shared suffering of watching others suffer. Why would we evolve like this in a random universe? Evolutionists posit that all that we are and all that we feel on some level enhances our survivability which in turn enhances our chances of procreation and dispersing our precious genes into the wild uncaring world. But suffering? How does that aid in stocking the gene pool and ensure future generations will be spawned acting as vessels containing our wonderfully unique genes?

Ah, then there's the opposing argument from the Creationist camp, the believers in The Pissy Old Man with a long white beard sitting on the edge of a cloud always scowling as if Noah's Arc is jammed up his

cosmic ass the intelligent design John Calvin Cotton
Mather camp they know why there is never ending
suffering it's because we deserve it! We are all tainted
by original sin (if we all have the same sin then what's
so original about it?) I bet I could come up with a more
interesting sin a unique truly original sin think of all the
possibilities a mobile art interchangeable Alexander
Calder Museum Of Sins the endless taboos the
countless breaches the ludicrous laws the delicious
violations violators will towed even better towers will
be violated turning the tables corrupting Satan tempt
him with an apple a big juicy Red Delicious Apple his
favorite or so I've been told by his indiscreet cronies
and shameless sycophants that Beelzebub is such a
chatter box flies coming out of his mouth as he gossips
I bet I could even outdo **Him Mr. D Himself** a little
brimstone a little sulfur a pinch of hell fire and a sturdy
pitchfork from Home Depot and watch me work. Sloth
Lust Envy Gluttony Wrath Pride Greed they could only
come up with seven where's Hate Deceit Vanity
Selfishness it's not nice to be shellfish said the minnow
to the crab you can only take one cookie from the
cookie jar take five talk loud at the library laugh in
church laugh like a contemptuous hyena laugh at the
priest with his jewels and robes his sanctimony
preaching the passion of the Christ as he thinks about
his passion for the boys despise the priest a sin or a
virtue? Oh so many fascinating sins fratricide regicide
my favorite patricide matricide no leave good ole' mom

alone she and I both hated the cold but I do have limits I will never drown all of humanity for not sucking up to me nor torment Abraham for the sadistic glee of it. It's freezing in Connecticut; better to rule in Hell than to serve in New Haven.

An idea. Don't dismiss this out of hand. What if ok call me crazy but what if the Red Wings were manufactured pre-scuffed? Don't scoff at the scuff. Like jeans that are pre-ripped which never made any sense to me but the pre-scuff would not be some pretentious fashion statement but an acceleration of comfort attainment both visual and tactile. Just a thought. What if there were some guy like me (I know I'm unique just like everyone else odd paradox) somewhere one in a billion chance but it's possible just like in an infinite universe there could be a planet just like ours which is actually more probable in an infinite universe than there being a guy like me in a finite world but if there is a guy like me with say a dormant affinity for Red Wings instead of waiting for the accumulation of scuffs if they're already there he could flop on the couch prop up his feet and presto he's ready to go.

The memories. The memories can be like ghosts haunting the mind and spirit. Like demons impervious to exorcism, openly mocking the priest with his holy water and crucifix spinning their heads around full circle within the child's body they possess, spewing

bile vile green vomit better duck uh oh too late your
face is a mess you've torn your dress or maybe it's a
robe try to wipe the loathsome green filth away as the
possessed child oh such a supple pretty little girl does
extreme backbends on her levitated bed and tells you in
a deep baritone that your mother sucks cocks in Hell.

But not all memories are bad. I remember her. Her
name was Sherry. She was beautiful. Long reddish
brown hair, light complexion. Almond eyes. Such an
odd expression. What challenged wordsmith came up
with that one? How about chestnut eyed Brazil nut eyed
pistachio eyed cashew eyed you get the idea.
Sometimes the best descriptions are comparisons.
Crack open your art books and put the nutcracker down.
Sherry was like the women from the Pre- Raphaelite
paintings. Lyrically tragic within an aura of blinding
color. She was intelligent in the extreme, a scholarship
student at USC. What did she ever see in me? There I
go again lethal low self-esteem thank you father you
did your job well you must be beaming wherever you
are hopefully in Hell.

We were both battered. She told me her father once
beat her so badly she was hospitalized for three days.
Her father had died shortly after I had started seeing her
(neither correlation nor causality was ever suggested.)
She loved her father deeply. She shouldn't have.
Women shouldn't love men who beat them. This
diminishes both the battered women and the men who

treat them decently but are ignored, for the decent should be respected more than the brutal. Here I go again- it's tangent time. I really can't help it. Women who react to their oppressors with love are flawed like whores who love their pimps like duplicitous slaves who love their slave masters obsequious in their treachery tipping off the overlord the rebellion will commence when the clock strikes twelve. Oh these digressions of mine. These annoying detours from my train of thought where is my discipline to reign in my wandering mind?

I lost my virginity to Sherry. She was patient with me. We weren't together long. Part of the end of one year, part of the beginning of another. But one memory. Early December. The sky littered with flowing, golden dying leaves. The Coliseum was next to the school. We climbed over a locked gate and walked up the Coliseum steps. The crisp desolation. No one in sight. We were like the last two left alive. The last breath of Autumn made the golden leaves swirl. We embraced and kissed. The scent of her as I lost myself in her hair my glowing tragic Pre- Raphaelite woman that moment forever etched in memory it may have been my finest moment my apex moment I knew it even then.

Memories are fleeting they tease and bob and weave in and out of consciousness like butterflies evading the net for fear of being pinned to the wax board. So many horrific memories perhaps repression is a gift a safety mechanism preventing freefall into madness. Nearly blinded oh dear sister never showing sorrow or remorse oh dear father your face beet red raw liver red as you beat me as you told me you cursed the day I was born you probably could have strangled me in the cradle my mother once told me I fell out of a bassinette as an infant do babies fling themselves out of bassinettes I prefer to think I was pushed surrounded by likely suspects we can eliminate the butler we didn't have one oh what a strange menage that would have been a dignified Jeeves in tux and tails wandering about the familial madness perhaps he would have taken pity on me and spirited me away sold me to the Gypsies or placed me in a basket left me at a random door with a note: *Oh please have mercy on this hapless child of misfortune.*

I stare at them. You know who or should know at this point. Them. My salvation. My Red Wings. There was an old lady who lived in a shoe. I hope it was a giant Red Wing with a skylight and indoor plumbing many beds and many baths she may have been old but with long lived fertility poor woman all those numerous children and not knowing what to do.

Why am I not in a state of dread or at least alarm by the state I'm in? This obviously is not normal by any wild stretch of the imagination. I haven't a clue how long I've been lying here nor do I seem to care. Do I eat food? Drink water? I should be in a state of panic, but as long as those Red Wings are in my visage I'm floating on a sea of tranquility.

There was a man. I remember. His name was Michael. Michael was older than me, much older, old enough to be my father. We were workmates working in an impossibly immense building, an inverted pyramid called the Ziggurat. It seems so strange, so long ago. We were working at a census processing plant as warehousemen; general factotums moving things around all types of things furniture boxes crates machines anything that was movable we moved by hand by pallet jack by forklift by dolly golly it was hard work. We would move things from a to b then back to a because there were planning errors bureaucratic boondoggles snafus indecisions bad decisions no decisions it was the federal government after all. Please don't get the wrong idea. I bear no grudge no truck no beef nor issue with the federal government as a whole look at the private sector by comparison so many diminish and vilify the government and lionize if not indeed deify the private sector anything the government can do the private sector can do better more cheaply less wastefully competition keeps them on their toes performance by God they must perform fast and efficient or fall to the wayside it's a dog eat dog world profit is the name of the game succeed or die. And that's why the private sector is so odious at least through the prism of my nostrils. Within the private sector one must bring home the bacon and guess who the piggies are you got it it's us we are the prey to be sliced and diced pruned and plucked conned and swindled we all have horror stories of being screwed by the plumber bilked by the mechanic hoodwinked by the car salesman (oh those car salesmen do take a thrashing from me!) swindled by the attorney and operated on by the surgeon whether we need it or not oh how convincing they are how authoritative with their deep sonorous voices and spotless white smocks oh those tonsils just have to go but my throat feels fine doc now now doctor knows best and while he's at it he may as well remove those pesky adenoids and since you're already anesthetized unconscious he's in there anyway let's go for the gallbladder the spleen you can get along nicely without either oh and by the way it appears you're not circumcised why in this day and age no better time than now you're never too old for genital improvement or is it mutilation just one little snip only hurt for a minute and studies have shown that women prefer men with that rabbinical look. What else? Any other organs not nailed down? They're cheaper by the dozen how about a prophylactic colostomy or a preemptive hysterectomy?

But the noble public servant is not motivated by greed and profit is honest no reason to bring home the bacon never why you'd think they were all vegan bacon never touch the stuff the public servant pure as the driven snow Johnny on the spot steady at the helm we aim to please through rain sleet and snow oh you bet yes sirree Bob!

Where was I? oh yes- Michael. Such a fascinating and complicated man. By turns suave, vulgar, urbane, crude, coarse and refined. A man of many hues a chameleon of sorts a conman man an exceptional man my confidant a man of many hats of many moods a world traveler a raconteur par excellence his stories rich and endless. He was a German born in America East Saint Louis his father murdered by a Black man or so he believed his mother remarried and he and his mother and step father moved to Germany then to England and back again to Germany and the full circle back to the good ole' USA.

Depending on his mood or circumstance his accent reflected all three countries and within a single statement he might vacillate from English to German to American with the accent of an English gentleman usually being dominant. He did various jobs throughout his life he was brilliant self-educated he finally found his calling as a purser for a major American airline. Do they still have pursers? I don't think so a good choice for him I suppose he could appear dignified aloof yes there was something of an English butler about him cool unflappable a Jeeves perhaps no- Jeeves was much too affable Michael could be cold and cruel Jeeves was benevolent solicitous Michael was the guilty butler who really was the murderer if to suit his purposes he would have shanked poor Bertie Wooster in the heart.

Oh the stories Michael told me some too fantastic not to be true. He used to smuggle gold watches from Switzerland I certainly wouldn't put it past him ah a purser what better front could there be it started with just a few then greed set in he was caught and nearly went to prison he had his small daughter look and behave like a hapless orphan at the trial and believed that got him off the hook. We once talked about the relativity of morality of one man's patriot being another man's traitor oh poor Benedict Arnold forever loyal to the Crown the great British patriot the vilified American traitor and what if King George had directed greater assets to squelch the rebellion could not Washington have wound up on the gallows his name synonymous with treason uttered with contempt by loyal men everywhere? It's all point of view we're all victims of circumstance pawns of fate molded by place and time.

One day Michael came to work with a packet of old photos of himself as a young man in Germany circa 1930's. In one pic he is standing with a group of other young men all of them decked out in full sartorial Nazi regalia standing proud in their smart uniforms swastikas

on their shirts and sleeves. I was dumbstruck. Michael
was a Nazi! Not some ignorant inbred American Neo-
Nazi of later decades but the real deal in the time of Der
Fuehrer! Then to ease my shock he explained to me that
this was an excellent illustration of the relativity and
subjectivity of morality. He calmly and logically
explained that if you were a red blooded patriotic young
German at that point in time being a Nazi was the thing
to do and not being one cast a shadow of suspicion and
yes this point in time was before Germany's defeat and
the taint of history the stigma of losers cast by the
victors slammed by the hammer of hindsight. In a sense
they didn't know they were Nazis not the ones we know
through the prism of time and victory. But oh what a
virulent anti-semite you were! So often when we spoke
you voiced your hatred, always in an eloquent dignified
way, not like some American skinhead of latter times
with a tattoo on his head his hand thrust in the air and
his head up his ass. You would have been an art and
Wagner loving Nazi you drank the Kool-Aid and loved
the taste if things had twisted a little bit differently who
knows oh how you would have made the Fatherland
proud.

Now where am I? Oh fickle, arbitrary memory
where have you taken me now? I'm groggy. Sleeping
on the job, perhaps. Something feels odd to my touch.
Whoa. **What's that in my hand! I** didn't put it there,

but if not me, then who? And now, gentle reader, a few profound and salient thoughts on masturbation.

I recall hearing from an "expert" that <u>all</u> men masturbate. I don't recall if <u>all</u> women do as well. (clarification: I mean if all women masturbated, not if women do it as well as men because they would of course do it better, having superior dexterity in things like knitting and sewing on buttons, and handling small diminutive objects in general.) Most male mammalian species masturbate except for donkeys, who have no opposing thumbs, which accounts for their horrible dispositions. There are thousands of YouTube videos featuring voluptuous young women wearing sprayed on leotards doing intricate contortionistic yoga postures. **Spoiler Alert.** Women don't watch those videos. In fact, serious yoginis are contemptuous of them. **Only men watch them.** Can you guess why? And are you aware that these videos are produced and financed by the American Association Of Carpal Tunnel Surgeons? Not to get tangential (as if I can avoid it), but not only do all men masturbate, but all men despise yoga as well. Men go to yoga classes for two reasons only: to gawk at voluptuous young women in sprayed on leotards doing splits, and to develop sufficient flexibility in their cervical vertebrae allowing them to perform autofellatio. Well dream on men. It will never happen, thus proving that all men masturbate, despise yoga, and are stupid as well.

Is masturbation a sin? An unnatural act? Well if it's unnatural, then why do all men do it? Even The Holy Roman Catholic Church has lightened up. For centuries, priests were told they'd go to Hell if they masturbated. Now they can- providing they use an altar boy's hand.

So there you are. Take it from an expert. Take it from me.

Now where are we? Ah yes. Driving. Traffic lights. We can't live with them and we can't live without them. But they have buttressed a long held misgiving of mine a belief easily dismissed as irrational absurd unscientific and mathematically impossible. The belief? The belief is that traffic lights are not what they seem. They are intelligent sentient discerning discriminating all seeing watching us as we watch them and oh they have their favorites they smile at some and beam good fortune green green always green for the chosen, green as the grass after rainfall green as cash fresh off the mint green as emeralds polished by master gem cutters green as envy yes envy is what I feel watching these lucky souls glide through intersections with eternal e-tickets it's a wonder they don't have their brakes removed who needs them anyway? I do. There are those who are despised by the traffic lights who are shunned shamed and cursed by them for no discernable rational reason. Those like me. It's not as if I have disrespected dishonored or denigrated those blinking winking shining sentinels of safety and order recklessly ignoring their authority plowing through intersections when the lights are red shining crimson scarlet red ruby red no it's something else perhaps prejudice for reasons even the towering traffic lights don't understand but I understand for I am the king of the accursed enemy number one for me there is one color only guess which one it's the color of blood and roses rubies and hellfire yes yes red red red interminably relentless red.

The left turn lanes are the worst the light is green I speed up yes for once I am going to make it buck the system unravel the natural order closer closer still green I enter the lane only three cars ahead but lo! All three make slow lazy u-turns and as the third one begins to turn the light turns red. Or, late for an appointment, I've got to make that light it just turned green just a little faster yes yes I'm almost there just one car ahead of me I will make it easily I pound the accelerator in the same instant the overly cautious driver in front hits the brakes oh how close I feel Mayhem's hot breath on my neck my eyes widen like astonished saucer plates I slam the brake pedal that sickening screech of wheels no longer moving but the car still does the stench of burnt rubber I stop an inch before I rear end the car in front no not yet not this time the traffic lights don't want to lose me they plan to keep me around for future bliss oh the

endless amusement I provide them as the light eternally
turns red just as I reach the intersection and the
innocent hapless souls behind me the collateral damage,
they also must suffer and when in the distant future
when the light turns green they will have nine inch
toenails spider webs in their nostrils birds nests in their
hair their mummified body parts torn off toted away
and tagged by eager young paleontologists.

Now what? And where? Where and in what
direction will the fluttering wings of memory carry me
and on what scarred ravaged landscape will I be
dropped? Again. Again the flight stops at childhood.
I'm nine in the third grade our teacher Mrs. Bloom has
taken ill for an extended period. We have a substitute
teacher she looks so young maybe fresh out of college a
neophyte thrust into the lion's den of vicious children
yes I said it vicious whoever came up with the notion
that children are sweet and innocent Goldilocks and
Little Miss Muffet Little Red Riding Hood skipping off
to grandma's with a basket full of goodies fairytales
such sugarcoated fairytales! For a more accurate
depiction see Patty McCormick in *The Bad Seed* or the
malignant young Darwinists in *Lord Of The Flies*. Oh
such darlings are children look at them play outdoors
the adorable way they rip off the wings of butterflies
and break the legs of beetles before placing them atop
ant hills oh how cute as they watch the small creatures

wiggle and thrash in torment oh listen to them giggle with sadistic glee.

Our substitute teacher immediately recognized me as a kindred spirit apart from the others we connected with invisible tendrils oh how my classmates tormented her it was her name that gave them license *Mrs. Smails* oh the chorus of malicious giggles why that sounds like smells. And so it began a refusal to accept her, disobeying, misbehaving at every turn who does she think she is she's not our regular teacher this imposter this interloper strength in numbers they attacked relentlessly, "Mrs. Smells, Mrs. Smells."

One day she asked me to stay after class for a few minutes and when the room was empty save for the two of us she broke down in tears "You're the only one who's good to me the only one" and like so many times before and since I felt another's suffering and wept another's tears and why oh why can't I do something?

Schools of thought. One school maintains that children who are abused by their parents are more likely to become abusers themselves when they are adults. The other school maintains that childhood abuse and trauma has a nurturing effect on one's empathy and compassion; that those who have suffered can relate to others who have suffered in a more heightened and evolved fashion. There once again is a nature vs.

nurture element to these theories. In the nature camp it is suggested there may be a genetic succession; abusers are inherently abusive and pass those loathsome genes on to their progeny. Or perhaps they're both right. Genetic predisposition toward abusiveness plus environmental imprinting i.e. my father is whipping me with a strap so this must be how I must behave like father like son the apple doesn't fall far from the tree here we go again banal clichés and obnoxious folkisms. Frightening possibility- what if it's neither nurture nor nature something beyond the genetic code beyond behavioral imitation something undetectable by blood tests or magnetic imaging cat scan or divining rod? Maybe we simply are what we are though far better than superstition and mumbo jumbo magic ah there is that arrogance in science that certainty that all effects are preceded by causes well don't stumble over that pesky primal atom I've evoked before where in hell did that omnipotent dot in the void come from you don't know caught you with your pants down here let me loan you my suspenders.

Have I mentioned that I wish I were a bastard? That my mother had had a fling with the mailman or the milkman or the handyman the gardener the vacuum cleaner salesman the butcher the baker the candlestick maker the dog catcher the organ grinder anyone other than my father, or that horribly narcissistic actor who does the Lincoln commercials (I suppose he's disqualified way too young to be my father but then again how the hell old am I anyway?) Oh how I would rejoice to know I'm not my father's son such a horrible thing to say you may be thinking surely even the worst of fathers at least have taught their sons some skills uh uh I remember my father trying to teach me to tie my shoes I was a little guy he got impatient after failing with my first try then said, "Do you know how to tie a knot, Stupe?" I meekly answered yes and he replied, "Then just put loops on the end of the laces and tie knots," then he stormed off. I never learned to tie laces the proper way (thank God those Red Wings are infinitely more tolerant and patient than my father.) Anyway, before I completely lose my train of thought, there's too much evidence to the contrary, even without DNA testing (although, just to be sure, it might be cathartic to exhume the old boy's body and test whatever may be left negative or positive no lingering doubts yay or nay the final nail in the coffin good God did I actually say that even I'm ashamed but he would probably say the same thing if he were witty, which he was not.) That stupid saying "The apple doesn't fall far from the tree (seems like the more contempt I have for a stupid saying the more likely I am to use it) well get a load of me when this apple fell it rolled and rolled defying physics it rolled and kept on rolling as if thrust by propellent leaving the tree way beyond the horizon. How horrible you must think I am harboring and fostering such venom for my father honor thy father oh

holy father you think I am a deranged man with
Oedipus issues Oedipus didn't know the half of it and
you obviously never met my father.

The tooth was loose. I was ten not too soon before
the bleeding began before my guts would sprout lesions
like stigmata. I had come home from school my mother
wasn't home but my father was, awaiting my return,
lying in wait. He seemed to rejoice upon my return, as
if I were the Prodigal Son. He seemed so damned happy
to see me. You'd think I would have learned by now,
that I would have bolted like a gazelle upon seeing the
lion's drooling chop licking leer. "Let me show you
something in the bathroom," he announced, beaming
with excitement. I followed him then when we were
inside he pounced, emitting that horrible giggle/squeal
sound he'd make when tormenting me. He wrestled me
to the cold floor, forced my mouth open, grabbed the
loose tooth and pulled. Oh how delightful to hear my
shocked holler, his sadistic juices flowing, ah rich
sweetness of fatherhood!
    Yes, I rolled far from the tree but my father's
branches loomed long oh please let there be a Hell with
my father sizzling in a special place of honor.

Einstein I've been told arrived at many of his
theories by daydreaming creating mind teasers almost
childlike a man riding on a beam of light or a passenger

on a train moving so fast time slows down picture book scenarios the scientific formulae would come later.

I remember I had my own physics mind tease. It came up in college between classes while smoking a joint with a friend lying supine beneath a tree looking back it seems we were always smoking a joint beneath a tree after all isn't that what college is for didn't Plato himself teach his students within a grove called *The Academy* so arguably we were classicists not doper slackers but practitioners of antiquarian learning techniques.

So here is our brilliant intellectually provocative scenario: A man is inside an elevator that has gone up to the fiftieth floor of a skyscraper when, poor hapless fellow, the cable snaps and he is in freefall. Well what if, just what if, at the split second before the elevator hits the ground the fellow jumps up and, for a nanosecond, is in midair when the elevator hits the bottom. Would he escape death? We chewed on our scenario dissected it approached it from different vantage points it <u>seemed</u> to make sense why not think about it yourself do you see any glaring fallacy? How exhilarating, cheating death with one little properly timed hop. And guess what? Providentially someone had dropped the school newspaper nearby and we picked it up and low and behold on the front page there was a feature story about one of the physics department's professors who had won an award or a grant or something prestigious and we thought what the heck let's pitch our theory to him who knows we might be onto something truly revelatory we might even garner our own awards become honorary physics professors even draw attention from the Nobel Prize Committee. We walked down the hill to the physics department and found his office and lo! He was actually in the middle of an experiment with a colleague as my friend and I unceremoniously burst in oblivious to manners and social protocols and we presented our theory. And oh that look of astonished contempt on his face forever etched in my memory as he curtly told us the hypothetical man in the elevator wouldn't survive he would be travelling at the same velocity as the falling elevator and he would go splat only a split second later than if he hadn't jumped and we could go away now and please don't return and the lesson learned is if you feel a need to display your stupidity don't do it to a physicist there are plenty of humanities professors around.

I understand. I understand how someone would easily dismiss me as mad and, being fair-minded objective incorruptible evenhanded and comfortable in my own skin I might agree. That's a boldfaced lie. I twist and writhe itch and scratch pummel and kick in my own skin desperately trying to get out. And who came up with that stupid expression, "Comfortable in your own skin?" As opposed to how one feels enclosed in someone else's skin? Admittedly as an expression it's not as stupid as "You get my goat" which ironically is so obnoxious that the expression itself actually does get my goat or at least would if I had a goat which I can't imagine avowed city boy that I am and <u>why</u> would anyone want a goat in the first place what purpose do they serve aside from making disgusting sounds and kicking why some people have actually died from a hearty goat kick it must hurt like hell especially below the belt no not the farm belt or the bible belt but the buckle belt which replaced suspenders thus irritating set in their ways farmers redundancy <u>all</u> farmers are set in their ways and prefer suspenders like they prefer bib overalls over tuxedoes maybe it's the farmers' way of getting back at elitist snobs like myself they keep goats for that sole purpose to offend the likes of me and my ilk but I haven't got an ilk just as I haven't got a goat maybe I did at one time God knows why but some farmer stole it thus literally getting my goat!

I really do understand and bear no resentment let alone malice if there are those who think I'm mad as in bat shit crazy with these uncontrolled tangents and my single minded obsession with my magnificent Red Wings and let's not forget dear old Dad yes I fully understand. Hey! I know what I want to discuss. I better get it down before I forget. Alternate realities. When I

watch football the play by play analyst will invariably
say something like, "Well, if they had kicked a field
goal instead of going for a first down on fourth and one,
and failing miserably to pick up one little yard, they
would have won the game." Well it doesn't work that
way you boneheaded ex-jock. You assume that
everything else that happened in the game after failing
to pick up the first down would have been exactly the
same. Every other play every other penalty every other
score would have happened identically. Uh uh. Had
they tried to kick the field goal everything subsequent
would have been different. The dominoes would start to
fall there's no way of knowing what may have
happened the field goal may have been blocked and run
back for a touchdown who the hell knows it's called
football not crystal ball that physicist mentioned earlier
would probably have more contempt for you than for
me so stop swaggering around in your gold Hall Of
Fame jacket and ostentatious Super Bowl ring and show
some humility.

Maybe I need a pet. It might be problematic as pets
need to be cared for and I it would seem am eternally
on my back staring at my Red Wings and even if I
could get up judging by the scuffs on my revered and
wondrous shoes I probably wouldn't be any more
conscientious about tending to a pet than I am to my
Red Wings.

Dogs. Dogs make wonderful pets. They are unconditionally loyal absolutely loving categorically devoted to us most of whom are egregiously undeserving of their love and adoration. Most dogs are better people than most people so said the wise man look at us with our wars purges holocausts pogroms persecutions prejudices inquisitions rapes murders and lest we forget our abysmal manners and lack of etiquette using the wrong fork to eat our salad ordering the wrong wine with our entre forgetting to curtsy refusing to bow stepping on feet speaking in tongues telling untruths screaming great lies bursting with pride and behaving like boors.

None of the above would ever be associated with dogs. They love us so dearly slathering us with love pure love sloppy drippy love hysterical with joy at the very sight of us smelling us with voraciousness lapping and licking us with slavish adoration yes I know you naysayers they do sometimes bite and bark the bark always bigger than the bite small imperfections flaws that only make them more endearing. Yes, there is nothing like a dog.

But cats on the other hand. Those hissing treacherous creatures blasé when we arrive home unappreciative when we feed and pet them as if it's their imperious due snapping at us scratching us surely they are pretenders vile venomous vipers masquerading as mammals what is their allure why do we put up with them what purpose do they serve other than meowing and making blood curdling screeching sounds dogs despise them what better recommendation to follow suit and I can attest to this: women who love dogs are more tolerant of men than women who love cats so next time the coyotes roam leave the door open.

I had two dogs. The first one I mentioned- sweet tragic Honeybee. My other dog could have been reincarnated from Honeybee. Her name was Cindy. My loving soul mate Cindy. I was nine. Before the bleeding. Cindy was a pretty little Cocker/Collie mix. She was shivering with fear in a corner of her cage at the pound when I first saw her. We connected instantly. Two frightened, sensitive souls in a brutal world. I rescued her and she was my best friend. When I became sick a year later, bleeding delirious sick, she stayed with me every minute laying by my side and does this sound sad perhaps pitiful I've always wondered if anyone ever loved me as much as she did I wish she could come back and be with me right now my wonderful dog along with my wonderful shoes we could be our own little family.

OK Red Wings. On guard. Pay attention. Inspire me to remember how the individual is absorbed by the crowd then loses his soul when the crowd transmogrifies into the mob.

That was quick. It came in a flash. Junior college
October long ago although I'm never sure about time
anymore. It's a special day. An important tumultuous
day a day of national protest a moratorium against a
war which war there have been so many like protesting
against a fire when the world has always been aflame.
These wars do seem perpetual gotta keep that Military
Industrial Complex percolating Ike of all people who
better to know than a general he's the one who blew the
whistle sounded the alarm forever war requires eternal
enemies so there we go again this time in South East
Asia.

I park my car in a neighborhood near the campus
and get out. I belonged to a group. An anti-war group.
We even had a name: The Omnibus Society, perhaps
the most insipid name in the history of protests. The
Omnibus Society a name that strikes fear into the
corporate war machine yeah sure we may as well have
been called The Teddy Bears For Peace. We had
prepared for this day planned and lay down a strategy
basically don black arm bands sit on our asses in circled
solidarity on the grass in peaceful passive protest in the
speakers quad Jesus we made Ghandi seem like a bad
ass street fighting man.

Perhaps providentially another young man pulls up
behind my car and gets out he is a big lumbering fellow

wearing a white long sleeved shirt and he approaches me and asks in hushed noncommittal tones, "What do you think of all this protesting?" I dramatically whipped out my black arm band tied it tightly to my arm like a tourniquet in case a counter-protester should shoot me in the shoulder and replied, "I will be joining the protestors." He paused then nodded with restrained approval or so I thought and we walked our separate ways to the campus.

My comrades and I sat in a circle on the grass our black arm bands like uniforms informing of who we were and where we stood. The voices of the scheduled speakers in spite of the microphones grew weak as we could sense which way the wind was blowing. The people in the crowd who were sympathetic grew increasingly passive and timid and as the tide turned more people arrived angry people members of the football team and veterans and the tension turned into hostility we were outnumbered and surrounded and scared a real life lesson- you have principles? Only if you stick your neck out; stick your neck out and the risk is that there will be someone who will want to lop off your head. Then, I spotted him in the mob. The lumbering young man in the white shirt I thought I saw him earlier through the corner of my eye silent at first but now plugged in as the mob grew uglier so did he in direct proportion the mob began screaming at us cowards traitors commies and the lumbering young man was the biggest screamer of them all. The mob was like a malignant flower blossoming open spewing hate, screams of rage primitive and tribal we were the other, harmless yet a threat within our withering circle we were challenging the edicts of the tribe providing comfort to the enemy a mob has no rules of engagement no morals no conscience the hatred was like a swarm expanding engulfing I looked at the lumbering young man in the white shirt he was now frenzied the loudest screamer of them all we felt lucky damn lucky to see the day's end and get out alive.

Do we change? Do we ever truly evolve as a specie? Are we really separate from the other creatures occupying our fair orb by more than a flimsy façade and frail veneer? We love to think of ourselves as not part of the animal kingdom but elevated, touched by God, but are we truly more than simians with opposing thumbs who through some evolutionary fluke learned verbal symbolic communication? So disillusioning. I once believed that as humanity progressed technologically we would commensurately progress morally but woe to the world look at what we've done instead of arrows we now use missiles in our genocidal pursuits. Other species. Other species are also brutal and savage but for the purpose of survival. The pack must feed the pack must defend itself from competing packs. Predators didn't choose to be carnivores they were never given the option of grazing languidly alongside their gentle herbivorous brethren, the lion

munching on grass beside his dearest old friend the
gazelle. No. They are hardwired to kill, they do it
because they must, not because they like to and they
can. And so arises the human trait of cruelty for the
sake of cruelty. I find myself drifting back to seventh
grade woodshop.

There is a man. He is big and completely bald and
his cruelty shimmers like heat like something molten
oozing from his pores. He is the woodshop teacher. His
name is Mr. Unger. Mean menacing German Mr. Unger
cold Teutonic sadistic Mr. Unger and the woodshop
filled with seventh grade boys seemed like it was also
filled with medieval torture devices vices clamps saws
pliers drills hammers we all cowered in terror and for
good reason.

This was a different time a time when teachers
could enact virtually any punishment corporal or
psychological which they eagerly did oh so gleeful in
meting out their punishments why, wasn't it true, spare
the rod, spoil the child as the saying goes this is going
to hurt me more than it's going to hurt you someday
you're going to thank me for this sounds a bit like dear
old dad. Wana bet? Someday we're going to hate you
for this there are people in this world who richly
deserve to be hated many more than we like to think.

The first day of woodshop Mr. Unger laid down the law the protocol the strict rules and rigid regulations of woodshop. Oh how he missed his calling he would have made a wonderful inquisitor he would have been a grand inquisitor who needs amateurs like Torquemada when there's Unger here are the canonical woodshop rules no talking when the teacher is talking no misuse or abuse of tools if a jack plane is placed blade down on the table the culprit will have his hand placed in a vice and tightened work areas must be kept clean tools maintained with care no cursing spitting laughing or breathing excess air or drinking excess water although the supply of air and water are limitless stupid rules petty rules rules that could easily be broken with one false move one slip of the screwdriver or the tongue rules designed to be easily and accidentally broken so inquisitor Unger could dole out his perverse punishments after all is he not entitled to his pleasures too the malignant bastard?

One day a boy named Sam a decent good kid inadvertently said something barely above a whisper when Herr Unger was pontificating about the nuances of the coping saw and der woodshop teacher nonchalantly walked over to Sam and grabbed his knee with a vice-like grip and Sam began to cry as Mr. Gestapo applied pressure it is humiliating for a boy entering puberty to cry and how I felt for Sam now part of the Brotherhood Of The Bullied but I'm not finished

yet a young boy named Steve on another day one arrant
little peep out of him when the great man was lecturing
about the joys of table saws it was a swat for Steve his
entire backside black and blue oh if only our parents
stepped in to intervene but alas this was a different time
in a different world. In a more just world we boys en
masse would have ganged up on Herr Unger secured
his wrists to the tightened vices then as a special project
gone at him with drills coping saws pliers the entire tool
chest and with great pride presented the various pieces
of him to the principal extolling the virtues of team
work.

And then there was Audrey, or Mrs. Stafford as she
preferred to be called. My ninth grade English teacher.
If I were to describe her as a psychotic bitch you might
think, oh God here he goes again doesn't he have
anything good to say about his teachers or authority in
general it always seems so negative. As well it should.
But psychotic bitch- isn't he engaging in hyperbole in
overkill gross exaggeration meanness of spirit hey that
ain't no way to treat a lady etc. etc. Yes. But I can
assure you oh gentle reader a lady she was not I'm
being charitable to a fault it really is the kindest most
positive thing I can say about her for indeed more aptly
she was a malignant sadistic cunt and a credit to the
school's faculty.

Mrs. Stafford was a strict disciplinarian not unlike the Bitch Of Buchenwald I wonder why she didn't lecture with a riding crop in her hand she really didn't need one she had her Harpy talons and her M.O. was that she was a hair puller oh back then back in the day I had a thick mop of hair atop my head which is an appropriate place as opposed to my palms people would talk and speculate I masturbated for hours particularly if the hair was green.

One day we were given an assignment to memorize the prepositions all twenty six of them and I drilled and drilled then came the day of reckoning she must have had this planned she called on me first I stood up and began my recitation under fire got them all except two not good enough she told me go outside with her behind a building where we couldn't be seen I'll never forget that fiery look of lunatic rage in her eyes she pounced on me like a rabid cat sank her talons into my hair and pulled and yanked with all her strength back and forth back and forth my scalp was sore for days how would my life have been different if I pulled her hair back pulled every strand out of her skull until she was bald and bleeding I might have been sent to reform school and emerged as a hardened criminal and then up the ladder of success to state prison maybe San Quentin sitting in the first row listening to Johnny Cash brag about killing a man in Reno just to watch him die god damn it it might have been worth it.

But not all childhood school memories are sad or horrific. I'm not a complete glass is half empty sourpuss. Let me jump back a few years to grammar school, not the grassless skull cracking one, but a different one I attended after we moved.

Starting in the first grade through the sixth, there was an annual talent show. And the performers were perennial, indicating either favoritism or a marked dearth within the talent pool. There was Nancy Wilson, a sweet, kind and unassuming girl who would do an acoustic guitar solo every year, and it was gratifying to watch her skills grow commensurate with her physical growth. And then there were the unicycle twins, brothers who came on stage like rats in heat, mean little bastards, ferret eyes gleaming as they regaled the audience by popping wheelies and myriad other acrobatic wonders. Oh how pleased they were with themselves, every succeeding year more obnoxious than the previous. And of course my favorite: Margie Hume. Starting in the first grade she would perform, a cappella, that wonderful song from *My Fair Lady,* *"Wouldn't It Be Loverly"* with an adorable Cockney accent, all the while dressed up in Victorian frump like Eliza Doolittle. Six years of it. Oh such a brave talented child. And with each year she sang with greater authority, taking ownership of the lyrics. And I must admit that by the sixth grade when her voice became throatier and breasts began to bud beneath her Victorian blouse, she began to excite me. And during her farewell performance when she came to the lyrics, *Lots of chocolate for me to eat, a pair of slippers to warm my feet,* I felt flush, and, oh gentle reader, a bit of ebony stiffened betwixt my legs, subtle and ephemeral perhaps, but there nonetheless. And as the years passed, I lost track of sweet Nancy and talented Margie. But the void that they left was partially filled, when years later, I learned that the unicycle brothers got run over by a truck.

I stare. I stare at my Red Wings propped up in their proper place their place of honor if they could speak what tales would they tell? Down to earth tales tales of the street of asphalt forests and pavement jungles, of curbs and cross walks, of cracks and crannies, of below the ankle twists and tragedies, big and small, of lost change, discarded condoms, wedding rings, lost love of lost souls always looking downward, hoping to find what they've lost, hoping for a miracle. I stare and stare memories rise from the depths, the deep unconscious, rising like slow ether, like ghosts from the grave.

Is life nothing but a memory, one long memory broken up into episodes? We remember the past and whether the recent past of moments ago or distant memories of decades long ago memories have a will of their own a shifting morphing will a strong controlling will. Fog shrouds what really occurred and who knows what that was there are no corroborating witnesses, no cell phone photos, no sworn depositions contained within the memory vaults. And truth itself may be a cloud, hovering in the sky, changing form depending on condensation and variants of the wind.

The wind takes me back. Way back. I'm five. There's a cute little Mexican girl my age who lives across the street named Laura. We sometimes play together. How long ago was this? It was so long ago people burned rubbish in incinerators. Every backyard had one. Brick and mortar, like outdoor fireplaces or barbecues with a grate that opened and closed a cremation oven for garbage spitting out ash and smoke soiling the air to the point that when we ran and played hard outdoors the air was so foul that our lungs would hurt when we took deep breaths. Incinerators. Every home had one, in some obscure, discreet backyard nook.

One late afternoon Laura and I were playing when suddenly she grabbed my arm and led me to the back of the incinerator where we could not be seen. She took my hand and slid it down inside the back of her pants. I was confused and frightened and tried to pull away, but oh such a strong and determined little girl she held my hand inside her underwear and told me to insert my finger inside her anus. I complied then removed my finger but she grabbed my wrist and told me to insert a different finger. Oh how lacking in resolve I was my will power not yet nascent and sweet little Laura single minded in attaining her goal. I told her it was getting dark and Disneyland was about to start on T.V. (in hindsight, and I swear that awful pun is unintended, this has got to be the lamest, most ludicrous excuse in the history of anal erotica in which to extricate oneself from an uncomfortable situation, particularly considering my evolving sentiments regarding "The Happiest Place On Earth" and my abject contempt for "Vanilla Land" as an adult.) But no, little Laura put her foot down and told me with no small degree of sternness that I could only leave after all five digits were separately inserted and so it was and not long thereafter incinerators were banned as a public health hazard.

And oh, gentle reader, I wish this lurid excursion down memory lane could end and be written off as a singular aberration but nay- there were other little girls with single minded proclivities similar to Laura's. Was there a grapevine, I now muse, were there beats from some primitive kindergarten tom- tom, perhaps incinerator smoke signals informing the future Girl Scouts Of America that I was the neighborhood digital lothario? And so it was under the legitimizing euphemism of "Playing Doctor" I was enlisted- no make that insisted- by other little girls who felt feverish and wanted their temperatures taken you know where: there was Judy, the girl next door, actually a few years older than I (naughty Judy!) who had her own personal rectal thermometer and insisted her temperature be taken multiple times (to rule out false reads) and once two sweet innocents in tandem corralled me in a shed and they actually brought sticks they had specially selected from God knows where, and oh, someone tell me, what did all this mean, to what did this portend? And who was the victim? All of us? None of us, tabula rasa children that we were? Well I'll tell you who it would be. Me! Whether I was blameless or not, and although there may not be destiny there are recurring patterns. Yep, it would be me. Lock the little bastard up and toss the key in the incinerator!

It's amazing the things that are dredged up from the dark chambers of the human psyche repressed memories dormant but forever vigilant lying in wait for that particular trigger allowing them to rear their ugly heads like periscopes rising from the sewer. Perhaps repression is not necessarily a bad thing but a safety mechanism allowing us to maintain albeit tenuously our feeble grip on sanity. Sanity. Can any of us be truly sane? The horrors of life are omnipresent ubiquitous surrounding us all without respite without succor relentlessly absurd indefatigably barbaric the natural organic horrors the plagues earthquakes floods famines pestilences fires hurricanes tempests tornadoes simply aren't sufficient no indeed we inflict upon ourselves far worse with wars pogroms holocausts plagues genocide rape murder mayhem to say nothing of the vicious bastards who step on our feet as they cut in front of us in line. All of which pales when compared to what we do to the entire earth oh how it saddens me to state the obvious but the world would be a far better place without us the air and the water would be cleaner an endless variety of species no longer endangered the soil no longer putrid from pollutants the ozone layer no longer thinned and punctured the hellish temperature no longer melting glaciers raising water levels causing endless forest fires oh yes my fellow simians hear my clarion call think of the whales washing ashore choking on plastics the carnage the disgusting road kill the stomach turning wet markets dog carcasses hanging on hooks pangolins slaughtered for their meat that alone could be a persuasive argument for our annihilation what vile psychopaths would want to eat a pangolin probably the same ones who burn millions of acres of rainforests to clear the land for condominiums the adorable little Koala bears falling off flaming trees fleeing for their lives but alas the flames are too quick and engulf the hapless little Teddy Bears of the majestic rainforests oh shame shame on us all quick press the button on the Doomsday Machine we've clearly worn out our welcome let us depart in one fell poof can you imagine the jubilation of the surviving flora and fauna oh poor tuckered out Mother Earth picture if you can a global block party thrown by the mice and the lizards the fish and the flies the elephants and the armadillos the entire panoply of genus phylum and specie the entire realm of the organic yes they wail in bliss roar with ecstasy bark with euphoria hyenas laughing themselves senseless the lions dancing with gazelles the rollicking rhinos the rabbits in rapture yes yes good riddance they bellow **Why we thought they'd never leave!**

A thought. An unnerving thought. What if my Red Wings are not authentic? What if they are counterfeit forgeries fake bootleg replicas? Not the real deal the genuine article certified authorized canonized true blue dyed in the wool or more appropriately dyed in the leather bona fide Red Wing shoes? Would it make a difference? Should it make a difference? An analogy: A man a true carnivore has a craving for a big thick juicy sirloin steak so he goes to a highly rated steakhouse a five star establishment is seated gives his order to the waiter or the server or whatever the hell they're called now who can keep up with political correctness run amok let's stick with waiter old fashioned boy that I am who if my life depended on it could not explain how flight attendant is more respectful than stewardess perhaps the former is more gender neutral and not to appear an insensitive brute I do applaud the fact that

'Old Maid" "Cripple" and "Wetback" have fallen out of favor hopefully to never return. (I know. Another nearly non sequitur tangent you've probably lost interest in my original thought. Something about authenticity, or was it steaks?) And in due course the waiter returns with a sixteen ounce sirloin broiled to perfection medium rare and this man cuts the steak and succulent juices flow from the meat and the aroma is transcendent he puts the piece of steak in his mouth and chews and oh like ambrosia on the hoof the finest most delicious transformatively satisfying steak he's ever tasted then when he's presented with his bill the waiter smiling sheepishly informs him that he was unknowingly part of an experiment control group double blind and guess what that indescribably delectable steak was in fact a simulation of steak consisting of genetically altered grains legumes and nuts so the question is begged: does it matter? If the experience was as good if not better than the real thing should he fret fume and grouse?

Of course he should! He was deceived hoodwinked in the name of science and so I beseech you oh Red Wings tell me you're not fake oh hell why do I even ask you could never do that to me.

Do I repeat myself? I don't mean to. I used to think that people who repeat themselves are boorish saying the same thing over and over again the same theory joke story anecdote again and again as if their every word has such import that they bear repeating so those magnificent words become indelibly etched set in stone in the listener's or reader's memory for ever and ever. My position has changed. Maturity breeds empathy and I now realize repeating oneself may be due to short term memory loss not unlike people who incessantly interrupt oh how rude and disrespectful but perhaps for some, thoughts are fleeting ephemeral beats among the synapses and if they don't express a particular thought <u>now</u> it will fall into an obscure crevice somewhere in that boney dome the cranium.

And so if perchance I'm not repeating myself allow me to opine about courage. In fact allow me to step it up and bring to the conjectural table something loftier than mere courage that top of the pantheon of human qualities- heroism. Heroism. Has there ever been a word a concept so inappropriately used and so much misunderstood? A football player makes a spectacular daring play in the final seconds of the game snatching victory from the jaws of defeat (another lame banal expression admittedly not as flamboyantly stupid as "You get my goat" but one entirely lacking in imagination probably coined by the same backwater cracker barrel Longfellow in bib overalls and there I go again with my snooty elitism and no wonder our rural brethren hate the likes of me and my kindred ilk.)

Where was I? Ah yes, pontificating on heroism what's so heroic about scoring a touchdown or sinking a hoop? Nothing. Those guys are paid millions for doing such things it's their job yet we persist in calling winning athletes "Sports Heroes." And how about that great pilot you know the one that Sully fellow whose plane malfunctioned and he skillfully landed the plane on the surface of a body of water saving all aboard about a 150 white knuckle panic- ridden souls including himself. But is that heroic? He would have done the same thing had he been alone in the plane he was saving his own life as well as the others and don't get me wrong I'm not trying to diminish his great feat, but really, what did he have to lose? A true hero or heroine if that's even acceptable these days I know here I go again perhaps it's deemed sexist in today's fluid societal rules of lexicon plus heroine sounds like a central nervous system depressant dangerous and highly addictive so let me withdraw (ha ha) from heroine and use hero in a generic sense inclusive of both men and women as well as non-binary individuals and of course all of our comrades in the LBGTQ community.

So what is a hero? Who would be a hero per my lofty standards? Someone who takes great personal risk to help or save someone else great risk as in life and limb sticking one's neck out when The Grim Reaper has just sharpened his scythe and has been snooping around your neighborhood asking about you. But even with that not all acts of heroism are equal. Consider this illustration: a child is trapped in a burning house and two men agree to risk their lives by charging through the flames to rescue the child. Rescuer number one is a healthy and happy twenty- five year old with a wonderful wife and child of his own and a promising career his whole rewarding wonderful life is ahead of him. Rescuer number two is a chronically depressed sixty- five year old with no wife or family no one who depends on him his future is behind him his ship has sailed he really has little to live for so which of the two is the more heroic who has more to lose? Well like duh I hope you don't have to put on your thinking cap and subject this question to extensive analysis but alas things are never as simple as they seem for some people would consider the twenty-five year old highly irresponsible placing altruism above the welfare and future of his own family and so as in so much of life you really can't win.

All right Red Wings carry me away to another topic another subject let's shuffle off no not to Buffalo I'm far too sensitive to the cold let's take a walk around the block but don't step on any cracks. Ah! Superstition always a fascinating subject that broken mirror that ladder in your path that black cat all harbingers of ill fortune and bad luck and then there are curses the evil eye the blasphemy of saying the lord's name in vain you will be punished you know how strict he is how vain vindictive and thin skinned he is you'd think he'd be more secure being omnipotent and all yet he is a jealous God omniscient he knows when you are sleeping he knows when you're awake he knows if you've been bad or good so be good for goodness sake.

Back to curses. Many believe in them, many don't, but are still afraid of them. Where do they come from? Who is the cursor, the one who got the ball rolling and for what reason? The urban legend the word of mouth the imperfection of oral history there was an aggrieved person or persons boundaries are set don't tread on my turf obey my rules don't utter my name or absolute hell will come knocking at your door.

Yes, superstition. After all this time all the progress at least in science and technology we have made during the last several millennia superstition and its various cousins the supernatural a belief in conspiracy theories etc. etc. persist and appear to be gaining steam. Just look at the Flat Earth Believers once a derided amusing fringe group have grown in numbers and influence in spite of overwhelming evidence the Earth is round as in sphere look at the photographic evidence amassed from space by the astronauts but hold on they say it's fake the astronauts were actors the moon landing never occurred if it had why didn't the astronauts prove it by bringing back some green cheese everyone knows the moon is made of the stuff or at least some kind of cheese. **Cover-up!** Neil Armstrong's actual first words upon stepping on the lunar surface were, "That's one small slice of cheddar for man, one giant block of brie for Mankind!" and not only that when they planted the American flag Old Glory on a stick why were the stars and stripes fluttering proudly in the breeze there is no breeze on the moon it has no atmosphere although it is rich in ambience and is still embraced by romantics and werewolves alike.

The Earth is Flat? Then why don't all of you Flat Earth true believers form a caravan of SUV'S and drive in one straight direction and fall off the edge thus proving your point and relieving all of us who are rational from having to endure you?

How distressing depressing and ironically boring that history really does seem to repeat itself the arrogance of ignorance rears its odious head time after time thinking it is competitive with or probably superior to facts and science. Reliable sources tell me that there are people more than you may think who believe that there is a conspiracy of influential people politicians moguls celebrities media elites globalists who have formed a cabal of Satan worshipping cannibalistic pedophiles operating out of pizzerias how can this be, well into the 21st Century a conspiracy theory of such flamboyant stupidity? They've got to be putting us on but nay they are deadly serious and I mean deadly they believe the cabal must be exposed assembled and publicly executed who needs evidence facts proof that's

for the hoity toity high falutin' scientific types no the
truth is not under the microscope or seen through a
telescope it's not in the lab or in the test tube look
elsewhere for the truth it's in the tea leaves the chicken
entrails the crystal ball rumor has it read it in a tabloid
ah for the good old days the witch burning days the
Inquisition days ah yes those inquisitors would know
how to handle Satan worshipping cannibalistic
pedophiles put them on the rack tighten the thumb
screws hoist them to the ceiling with their arms tied
behind their backs oh those Medieval monks were such
a playful bunch giggling as they plied their craft science
is the true Devil's handiwork throw Galileo in the
dungeon make him recant heresy such heresy the Earth
and the other planets revolve around the sun
Blasphemy! The Earth is the center of the universe the
sun and the planets revolve around the Earth how do we
know tell us you inquisitors inquisitive minds want to
know reason is a dangerous thing the Earth is stationary
solid in the center of the universe and oh by the way it's
as flat as a pancake.

Is it telepathy divination or madness? I hear the
wisdom of the Red Wings they speak but they have no
mouths they see but they have no eyes but they do have
souls sorry about that groan if you will pelt me with
rotten tomatoes in a prior incarnation I may have been a
stand up comic a vaudevillian uttering horrible puns
and dodging hurled items it's a rough crowd out there

they have no appreciation of subtlety ah yes a microcosm of the world at large although some societies are more receptive to humor than others do the Saudis have comedians how about Isis those madcap zany fanatics what would one even sound like "Take my life- please!" or "Good evening ladies and Jihadists I just decapitated a hundred infidels and boy are my arms tired!" I don't mean to beat up on our wonderful Jihadist friends but talk about a group devoid of a sense of humor a French magazine does a caricature of Allah and the cartoonist and the entire editorial staff get assassinated say what you like about LDS but when the play *The Book Of Mormon* was released lambasting Joey Smith and his angel Macaroni or whatever his name was the Mormons took it as good sports never occurring to them to run amok and lop off heads but listen to me oh how I digress I was talking about my dear old Red Wings communicating with me sans speech code or sign language. Maybe. Maybe we're kindred spirits with scuff marks and scar tissue in our guts on some transcendental wavelength.

Alright. Maybe I should avert my eyes. I never really know in what direction my leathery friends will send me. Here it comes off I go I was hoping they'd let me off the hook on this one but evidently they are proponents of tough love.

Women. It seems so remote so long long ago and probably was as mentioned I'm not entirely sure how old I am myself the numbers seem to roll around as if in a slot machine or gaming table the roulette wheel black jack bingo Chinese checkers Parcheesi hop scotch or whatever else they do in that vulgar Nevada town. In any event you're only as old as you feel so I guess I'll be 132 on my next birthday.

Women. There were a number of them and there were times more than I'd like to admit when the crucial moment came (oops arrived is a better choice of words) and closing the deal escaped me. Isn't it refreshing to hear a man admit such a thing so unlike most take that famous basketball player for example who claimed to have had sex with over 20,000 women (yep that's not a typo) in his lifetime. If he died at seventy that would be 285.71 per year providing he was precocious and began fornicating at birth oh such robust virility I imagine neither Swiss Cheese nor the Crack Of Dawn would be safe around him. And when I faltered they (the young women) would look at me with large compassionate eyes and say, "Oh it doesn't matter silly, it's not that important." Yeah sure. Then why did I evaporate from the date list shuffled off to that Siberia for the flaccid oh the infinite cruelty of the distaff ones far better the Gobi Desert or Guantanomo but much too good for me off to the gulag in the frozen hinterlands a gulag for the limp perhaps the rationale being if it should pop up maybe the hapless appendage would freeze stiff.

Women. Young women. There is sexism and there is reality. Men and women are essentially different hence the differentiating nouns. Most young men are driven by sex. Opinion. Most young women are driven by it more. Old saw: men express affection to women in order to get sex; women provide sex to men in order to receive affection. Are you a man reading this? For that matter is anyone reading this? Well, scoff if you will. Have you ever been in a group with a more or less even mixture of men and women- perhaps in the workplace- perhaps in a social setting, a picnic or other outdoor gathering, and present are decent caring steady solid young men and then some asshole on a chopped motorcycle wearing a black leather jacket is introduced and the young women hearing the call of the wild listening to the drip of their hormones converge upon the **Bad Boy In Black Leather** their eyelashes fluttering hips wiggling tails wagging look at him the alpha male maybe he would hurt them sexually and as for those steady eddy lunch box bearing boring men ignore them or worse treat them with contempt. And so I stick my neck out. There are words that need to be said but are silenced stopped gagged here they are: there are two kinds of misogynists- men who are inherent asshole bullies who mistreat and are contemptuous of women and then there are the good decent sensitive men the men who would be good friends and great husbands who are shat upon by young women in favor of the black leather jacketed bad boys. The good men, the potential loving husbands and fathers are inspired to become misogynists for good men can only take so much. So there. A thesis open to rebuttal if in fact anyone actually reads these tangential stream of consciousness rants. No. I'm being hard on myself. Postulates, that's what they are, provocative postulates incorporating logic and critical thinking.

Speaking of which. Logic and critical thinking. If I'm looping back a bit and covering some of the same territory as in Superstition vs. Science forgive me, not that I particularly want or need your forgiveness I rarely beg and if I did I doubt it would be for your pardon.

Once upon a time boys and girls before the internet spawned a plague of stupidity where every yahoo and his brother could render unto print any vile fatuous obscene hateful rave diatribe manifesto theory etc. ad nauseam there was a filtering mechanism editorial review percolation process which ferreted out the loonies goonies moonies and fruity tunies from being published in newspapers magazines books tomes scrolls pamphlets parchments billboards and prescription labels. The written word was first submitted then analyzed for truth accuracy interest relevance and yes logic before it went to press and the process could take days weeks months and perhaps years before the words could be read perused challenged rebutted digested or regurgitated by the public. There was peer review and there were consequences for lies exaggerations or even errors. Ah but double edged progress now in the electronic computer age the world wide web age anything is allowed any moronic psychotic lies and hallucinatory false-hoods can appear almost instantaneously on a screen for the entire world to see.

It sometimes seems that logic and critical thinking have been inflicted with stigmata in today's climate. Speaking of climate changing climate harbinger of death climate the climate change deniers are a prime example of logic and critical thinking bleeding at the wrists nailed to the crucifix oh such a heavy cross to bear for the reason lovers the science lovers the fact embracers the truth seekers when will reality be accepted it might be too late maybe when the naysayers burst into flame when they step out the door but will they accept the cause? Man-made fossil fuel emissions coal burning tail pipe belching smoke stack erupting man? No. It will be perceived as the will of God who's to argue with the man upstairs and isn't the end near anyway says so in the bible relax be good obedient subservient to the lord above tithe eat your spinach say your prayers atta boy atta girl play your cards right and you'll be sucked up to heaven in the rapture and the science people the logic people the critical thinking people will be left behind the smart shall inherit the earth and the righteous shall be lobotomized in heaven.

Snap out of it. Not you. Me. These reveries these flights of fancy these sojourns of cognitive anarchy one thought begets another thought theme theories rants raves opinions jeremiads mea culpas confessions careening off one another pinballs in an undersized pinball machine crowding one another elbowing jockeying for position inside my head. Hand me some aspirin shoot me some botox my head is about to explode then- then I refocus my thoughts my gaze I'm back to you my mighty Red Wings calm me sooth me talk me down.

And so they do. There was a day. When I'm not sure but I do know it's October. October, my favorite month more of a place than a time the month that has become a personal myth my own private El Dorado the month that envelops the best of my memories the month that transcends time yes it's a place the finest of places the warmest most golden of places as well as a state of mind.

How old am I? That place again between childhood and manhood where innocence is not yet dead but suspicions of reality have begun. I'm walking along a tree lined road. Trees endless trees a canopy of trees exploding in color trees leaves golden crimson yellow bronze orange crackling like static in the October breeze gaining momentum into the October wind. I'm surrounded engulfed by the extravagance the embarrassment of riches the bold audacity of color embracing me leaves falling swaying like parachutes lazy in the air like snowflakes on fire.

The wind becomes emboldened gaining force whiplashing through the trees the writhing trees the bending undulating tumultuous trees the leaves no longer gently falling now a blizzard a wild kaleidoscope of color flaming color blinding color- then she appears.

She appears from nowhere as if indeed blown in by the wind. She appears about my age, no longer a child, not yet a woman. She's beautiful, ethereal, her hair red rouge red scarlet and exploding from her head, wild tendrils jettisoning to the sky, wild and reaching, grasping the wind pulling at the wind she is the wind and she approaches me and takes my hands in hers and we dance.

Her pale skin alabaster skin large green eyes smiling eyes we twirl in our dance twirling spinning dervishes in the wind faster and faster we go in rhythm with the wind the manic wind the insane wind faster and faster until we rise with the wind ascend with the wind taking flight with the wind we are the wind.

Alright. Maybe that's not a memory. In all honesty it's a fantasy. But it should have happened. And if I go back to it again and again then in a sense it is a memory- a memory of a fantasy, but a memory none-

the-less. Ah to be carried away by the wind hand in
hand with a beautiful wind sprite no longer a child but
not quite a woman to be whisked away have I spoken of
this before this notion of the wind as liberator breaking
me out of the internment camp of life? Yes. I can't help
myself. There will be no deletions.

My father. Again and again I keep coming back to
him. Should people let go? Let the nightmare past slide
into the subconscious, purge the memories of events
dwelled upon that can't be changed? So difficult to
forget, more difficult to forgive, when no one ever
expressed remorse- no one ever said I'm sorry.
Closure? Maybe it's just not in the cards.

What if? What if my father and I could meet mano
et mano both of us in our respective primes hand to
hand combat on an even playing field his parental abuse
vs. my unbridled rage who would emerge victorious the
smart money on him and why not it's not as if he hasn't
beaten me before but that was then he was a man and I
was a child he was my father honor thy father an edict
undoubtedly forged by a father oh father why hath thou
forsaken me and I the son an avenging prodigal son the
forever wounded son give me strength oh stalwart Red
Wings allow me to mete out justice to hell with justice I
want revenge Revenge **is** Lady Justice before she puts
on her make-up justifiable patricide I want to see him
cower I want to see him bleed.

Or. Or we could talk about it. Why he may have had a damn good reason –"Well son it hurt me more than it hurt you and it was for your own good spare the rod spoil the child the fact that you were a good boy and really did nothing wrong is hardly relevant now is it?" Some people say the past is over let go of the rage the hurt the hate I don't want to let go you should never let go you never know what you might fall into let him make the first move his ghost might be a better man than he was.

For a long time now I've harbored a nightmarish thought. The thought? That any horrific thing you can conceive of capable by human beings has been done. The most extreme tortures cruel carnages unspeakable perversions have happened. Whatever your sick and wild imagination can conjure has at one time occurred. That thirty year old man still being nursed by his mother the experimental dismemberments without anesthesia people impaled by bored potentates acid thrown randomly in the faces of innocent people walking their poodles, all of it and much much more. So be careful what you think.

Is it really? Is it really that bad? I look at the world look back on my experiences I look up and down in and out I look through the window out the door up the skirts down the blouses I walk behind marching Scottish bagpipe bands with mirrors on my shoes the better to

look up their kilts. I can't help it I see bad things
everywhere people doing horrific things to one another
dog eat dog the bites always worse than the barks which
reminds me the Right Wing people (not to be confused
with the Red Wing people who represent a rarified class
of highly refined morally evolved individuals) the anti-
government people the laissez faire people the get
government off our backs people the Social Darwinist
people they believe in dog eat dog unless of course
they're the dogs getting eaten that's different lay out the
safety net throw the life preserver call the dog catcher
for god's sake bring on the govment'!

There are people. Many more than you may think.
People who can't sleep. Caffeine? No. Sleep apnea?
No. Eating before bedtime? No. Snorting near lethal
amounts of crystal meth at midnight? No. **The Great
Asteroid** making a beeline for planet earth? Yes.

There are people obsessed with The Great
Asteroid. It's out there and closing in fast. They lie
awake at night, staring at the ceiling, eyes wide like
saucer plates of angst, their bedclothes drenched in
sweat. Why? Why worry about something that is
immeasurably unlikely to happen within the next billion
years? The dinosaurs didn't worry and look where they
are now (oops, fell into that one.) But having brought
this up, there are people who deny the existence of
dinosaurs. There were no such creatures because fossil

evidence is fake and they're not mentioned in the bible. The arc could never accommodate them, not even one, let alone two of every kind, plus it's a known fact the earth is only 6,000 years old and flat to boot, just put a level on the ground if you want proof but I digress as I inevitably do. Back to the Great Asteroid neurotics. The people who never worry about death by cancer or traffic accidents or homicide or slipping on banana peels and breaking one's neck (slipping on a banana peel never results in a minor injury it's breaking one's neck or nothing) or psychotic spouses rabid dogs lunatic clowns lightening striking twice in the same place plagues pandemics terminal restless leg syndrome uncontrolled GERD the clumsy wife who drops a plugged in heater in her husband's bath (he deserves it men should never languish luxuriously in a tub they should confine themselves exclusively to showers) old age or simple natural causes while sleeping peacefully surrounded by loving family (which sounds like an oxymoron a fate worse than death as I imagine checking out surrounded by my family). But they can't get their minds off that asteroid.

There could be trillions of them in an infinite universe floating around near the speed of light willy nilly cosmic pinballs no rhyme or reason one knocking into another changing course careening helter skelter onto a pathway to Earth unstoppable inexorable where's Bruce Willis when we need him there look up in the sky it's a bird it's a plane no it's **Super Asteroid** looming larger every day until it swallows the sky then boom the world and all its myriad denizens pulverized evaporated could be a blessing in disguise no more migraines traffic jams bankruptcies hemorrhoids boorish offensive neighbors a final cosmic analgesic just ask the dinosaurs they have no worries.

The search. The quest. Should I be out and about looking for something? I look at my Red Wings up on the couch. What do you think, Red Wings? Sometimes they can be so inscrutable. Why not? Why not go out maybe a treasure hunt might do me some good. Ah the versatility of Red Wings they're not just excellent work shoes but also darn good walking shoes maybe they need to get out as well a little fresh air and exercise hard to know they ain't talkin' they can be so aloof at times pros and cons they might feel rejuvenated perhaps even liberated hitting the old pavement once more but then again they might step on something unpleasant there are dogs out there with cavalier owners derelict in there doggy dew disposal duties or worse yet gum now that would be an effrontery to their sensibilities for they are shoes of substantial dignity.

Some people believe life itself is a search some know exactly what they're looking for clear delineated goals with each step in their journey they're a little bit closer others feel a void they want filled a spiritual cavity that must be filled and so they search intrepid not knowing what they're looking for but hopeful they will know it when they see it.

I'm drawn. Drawn back to a place of dread and horror. Oh Red Wings why? Why have you directed me guided me back to the worst days the darkest days of my life?

I'm lying on my back. A frightened eleven year old hemorrhaging inside guts inflamed on fire no hope no love no friend advocate protector. Was my mother around? Yes. I grew to understand her more she would hold me when the pain was greatest she was overwhelmed by it all her life the way things are she too was afraid of my father. How many? How many blood transfusions did I have how many desperate hours staring at the ceiling?

They come. Yes, I've mentioned them before but they keep returning in memory never satisfied insatiable for –what? What did they really want? They come daily in a group with a cart loaded with folder case studies I'm in the pediatric ward the glass wall facing the hall all glass a fish tank of sick and suffering children glass all around so they can observe and discuss and take notes. Interns. Young interns cold eyes focused on me studying me analyzing me their fascination is in the disease not the treatment. Was there a treatment besides the arterial refills they whisper I can see but not hear their whispers their observations then they move on to the next child oh so many of us it's called euphemistically a teaching hospital but who is the teacher and who are the taught we're lined up in a row cadavers that can still wiggle still breathe still cry still scream we should have been paid why we're worth our weight in gold.

My father. Who art in hell if there is a hell beyond the one right here. He blamed me for my sickness my pursuit of self-improvement my modest exercise regimen and healthier diet you may be thinking no you're dyslexic he blamed you because you refused to exercise and your diet was unhealthy nope you read it right he had to place the blame away from himself I made my bed now I must lie in it even the doctors no friends of mine told him he was in fallacy land had I done nothing different from before except for the wearing of yellow and purple socks he would have blamed that, "Your fault Stupedo look at those socks!" He had no health insurance for his family what to do with me the unholy bargain the "Teaching Hospital" the euphemism for charity ward we'll take him in but for a price we don't want to cure him or treat him we want to observe and barely keep him alive after all he's no good to us dead.

Then. Then one afternoon after four weeks I saw him for the first time.

Black man. Black man with a mop. He seemed old to an eleven year old but was probably around thirty. He was a custodian. He would go up and down the hospital halls swinging his mop in a figure eight rhythm with a stylish flourish and a subdued low key swag. Black man with a mop. Every day when he passed my room he would glance at me the suffering boy the struggling boy the bleeding from inside boy and one day he stopped mopping and walked into my room he was kind he was well spoken he was compassionate and he spoke with me. I had never spoken with a Black man before he was unlike what I had been taught what I had been brainwashed into believing what a Black man was. He stopped by daily to offer me hope and encouragement he knew suffering he knew torment and injustice the knowledge was in his bones in his blood in his history and in his soul and as the days passed I would feel at least a little bit better his compassion more effective treatment than the cold stares through glass walls I wished how I wished for health I wished for an end to my agony I wished the Black man with a mop could have been my father.

Fathers. There are men. There are men who love their fathers more than they love God. There are men who think of their fathers and get tearful from their wonderful thoughts of their wonderful dads. There are men who learned all of their skills how to build things fix things invent things how to drive a nail how to drive a car how to drive a golf ball (oh and by the way not to digress but golf is the most preposterous game ever devised a pastime for the indolent bourgeoisie the morbidly obese presidents the snobs elitists nouveau riche the proudly disgusting who plant their fat asses on electric carts too lazy too unfit to walk caddies like sherpas carrying their golf clubs for them they may as well carry these arrogant lard butts atop their shoulders on gem studded thrones in a civilized society all the holes in all the golf courses would be filled and the lush green grounds converted to municipal parks.)

Ok. Where was I? Oh yeah, fathers. God was a father. He was an abusive father of cosmic proportion. Have you read your bible have you really read it and thought about what it says or merely accepted with large docile idolatrous eyes with puppy tail wagging submission how strict can a father be? So strict as to commit genocide on all of the men women and children on the face of the earth because they weren't sufficiently sucking up to him oh except for one Noah was adequately sycophantic and was spared but God wasn't going to make it easy for him you betcha he had to build an arc of specific dimensions and then stuff two of every kind of animal inside my what a tight fit God could have at least given Noah a shoehorn or some lubricant at least for the elephants and when God got tired of listening to the screams of drowning children he turned on Abraham with sadistic mind games go forth Abraham murder your son to prove you're loyal to me no wait are you crazy you're really going to do it your own flesh and blood what the hell kind of a man are you anyway? Does the other guy treat us that way you know who I mean the guy with the pitchfork the guy encouraging us to eat our fiber an apple a day keeps the doctor away? And when God looks down on us from above we appear as ants crawling wiggling insects despicable little creatures let me show my love for you sayeth the lord here have a plague still some of you left eh well here's a little pestilence to go along with that plague and how about some wars to stir up the pot what was I thinking when I created all of you if I could I'd give Adam his rib back and render him back to clay and why can't I if I'm omnipotent and if I'm omnipotent why the hell did I need to rest on the seventh day remember father knows best and you better give me something extra nice for Father's Day or I'll make history repeat itself open the flood gates crush the levies and the dams and this time my children my docile idiotic children invest in some lifejackets or at least in some straightjackets oh such fun to drive you all to madness.

And so. And so my own father was actually God-like in his behavior cruel nay make that sadistic

punitive when I never did anything to warrant
punishment just as the innocent children didn't deserve
to drown irrational impulsive acting on whimsy why
not? Who to stop him? A man's home is his kingdom
and he is the king and the king can behave as he pleases
look at ole' Henry you know the eighth one the one
with all those wives bear me a son give me an heir do
as I say or it's off with your head yes just like God
would do and all those men who worship their fathers
their strong wise benevolent fathers ah such irony how
antipathetic those fathers are to God paternal heretics
what a temptation to God to get inside their heads like
with Abraham and if those fathers were submissive to
the will of God and it was not a test what teary eyed
memories would you then have of dear old dad?

Where now my leathery spirit guides my muses my
partners in crime? What large cosmic issues can we
explore now what great celestial mysteries and enigmas
can we take a crack at solving what absolute truths can
we debunk what myths and legends can we expose
what charlatans can we deflate what icons can we
shatter but wait: even if we could should we? People
need mysteries and myths and legends they need
monuments and idols strewn about the landscape of
their iconography they need something to cling to
something to make life more interesting more endurable
don't be cruel and burst their bubbles what a dull
meaningless world without Bigfoot, Nessie, flying

saucers, The Fiji Mermaid, Piltdown Man, alien autopsies, Area 51, Elvis still lives and hangs out with Jim Morrison (The King having always been a closet admirer of Morrison's injection of Jungian symbols and archetypes into The Doors' music) dragons, giants, Easter Bunnies, Tooth Fairies and I'm just scratching the surface.

People need to yearn for a sense of wonder for a sense that skeptics are deniers or worse deceivers they know that remarkable things and creatures and persons are out there off in the shadows waiting for the right moment to reveal themselves to show their colors or in some cases to remain mysterious unsolved unseen unheard. D.B. Cooper hijacked a plane demanded a fortune in cash and four parachutes one for himself and one for his three hostages never intending that they would jump with him no if he demanded only one for himself it might not open oh such a clever man he jumped wearing a business suit and into the cold November sky over rural Washington did he pull it off was he a madman or a mastermind the two are not mutually exclusive do we truly want to know if he pulled it off or perished all this time no body ever found or perhaps better to forever wonder he left the earthly bounds and became a myth part of the collective folklore providing us with a sense of wonder, and strangely, hope. Why couldn't we ever do something like that?

And then there's the escape from Alcatraz. Frank Morris and the Anglin brothers creating dummies of themselves to fool the guards at bedtime (oh those wonderfully vigilant caretakers of our great public enemies with their keen observational skills never wondering why the heads of the escapees suddenly looked like coconuts) fashioning a raft from inflated raincoats did they pull it off paddling frantically with makeshift oars rowing through the frigid water of Frisco Bay their bodies were never found perhaps their bones lie beneath the sea sardonic smiles etched upon their boney faces well it was worth a try fun while it lasted or maybe they made it changed their identities became stockbrokers mailmen circus clowns vacuum cleaner salesmen or even men of the cloth comforting the death row inmates at their time of greatest need oh those prison guards gosh I could have sworn I saw that priest somewhere before of course you did at the produce stand where the coconuts lie let us conjecture let us surmise we need men (yes, yes, and of course women as well) with panache cojones resourcefulness men who say fuck you to authority and become part of the mosaic of legend for evermore.

Resolution. Closure. The tying of loose ends. Are there people so deluded that at the end they believe there was a grand scheme to it all and they figured it out? Suffering. All that suffering since the dawn of time

since the evolution of consciousness and nerve endings
since we crawled out of the primal ooze and looked
about with wonder and with horror. Why? What was
the meaning to it all? I wonder. I wonder if we all suffer
to a greater or lesser degree? I have known people. I
have known people who seem to glide through life
unscathed by suffering born into families brimming
with love and wealth moving from infancy to adulthood
to dotage the roadway always paved for them never
being allowed to fail or get sick or to lose in love in
profession in dice duels or dog racing always placing
their bets on the right horse the right stock serendipity
rendering risk irrelevant all sensations are good
sensations Seventh Sons of Seventh Sons seven
hundred dollars sewed into their pockets savings
accounts also accruing the highest rate of interest taste
buds primed for the finest foods gullets savoring the
finest wine loins destined for the finest sex yes I've
seen them navigating from a to z from birth to death
dying in smiling stupidity never knowing the true
nature of things.

And for the rest of us? For those of us with sadistic
brute fathers and hateful siblings our nerve endings
magnets for suffering our paths paved with broken glass
and hidden bear traps feeling the full brunt of sickness
Lady Luck getting her monthly at the mere sight of us
the drooling Fates licking their chops at the mention of
our names what of us of the short straw the snake eyes

the open sores the unlucky lottery ticket giving our neighbors license to stone us to death what the hell they've always wanted to regardless of our demises' effect on the corn crop let he who is without sin cast the first stone and all the saints rush to the quarry to find the best stones not too heavy to hurl but heavy enough to maim to kill bullseye and our brains drip out of our shattered craniums watch your step slaughter is slippery when wet so tread ever so softly on this treacherous landscape.

Ah yes. Treachery. We will all be betrayed it goes without saying some more than others it's just a matter of time and degree everyone we encounter is a potential son or daughter of Judas some people will do anything for thirty pieces of gold or was it silver guilt overwhelmed by gild shame outshined by greed ah yes indeed deceit and treachery hiding behind a smile lurking within a handshake promises, broken contracts, breached agreements sign on the dotted line ignore that small print it's standard boilerplate now turn over the deed to your house sucker the keys to your car and don't forget the pink slip.

Treachery. Gradations of treachery different kinds different motives from the careless benign to the malignant sadistic you tell a secret to a friend just between the two of us oops a slip of the tongue a lapse of the brain an accident no real harm done ces't la vie but rumors do spread one secret betrayed spreads like wild fire an innocent breach of trust now the entire world knows you wear women's underwear when you have sex with your dog but then far worse the big treacheries the dagger in the back treacheries the et tu Brute treacheries blood is spilled and entire armies have their positions relayed to the enemy resulting in large scale massacre treachery watch your back keep your head on a swivel you can't be too careful these days paranoia is not a myth when backed up by consequences an ally today could be tomorrow's deadly enemy just look at marriages true love absolute devotion in sickness and in health a year later the bride and groom are at each other's throats in divorce court the honeymoon is over try not to get cynical now.

They. You know They the amorphous faceless proverbial They as in They say a man is as good as his word that breakfast is the most important meal of the day They absolute authoritative They it's a known fact They- don't question They who says They say.

Think about it. Think of how docile you have become obedient never questioning oh what a wonderful dog you would be who's a good boy come on man up gird your loins authority was made to be questioned and if you don't like the answers the authority might, just might, need to be defied.

Think. Think about it. How many times have you heard, "We had no choice- we had to do it." But They never tell you what dire thing would transpire if They didn't do it or, "It's a known fact," well according to whom I bet you can guess or, "Why do we do it this way? Because it's always been done this way." What of it? Tradition is no indicator of validity and then of course, "We're all reasonable people who can disagree on many things but of course we all agree that..." do we why of course it doesn't even warrant discussion we all agree that what's good for Wall Street or Israel or Ford Motors or The Medical Pharmaceutical Health Insurance Monolith or The Military Industrial Complex is good for the United States and what's good for the United States is good for the world.

It's a known fact. A given. Self-evident so let's not think about it. That's what They say.

All right Red Wings cut me some slack let my mind catch its breath let me relax and just gawk at you perched up upon the couch let me just stare at you unburdened by thought and reflection. No dice huh? OK have it your way.

Slavery. Are we not all slaves on some level and to some degree? We take orders all of our lives from parents teachers bosses cops captains generals and if we rebel there are consequences parental restrictions detentions tickets terminations court martials

imprisonments executions racks thumb screws
floggings flailings and even severe scoldings so behave
yourselves watch your manners hold your tongues don't
talk back hop to it salute curtsy bow kneel don't sass
back pull over when you see red lights flashing in your
rear view mirror and sirens screech keep your hands on
the wheel is there a problem officer yes sir no sir what's
that you say sir I didn't signal when I turned but officer
I never turned the road is straight for twenty miles
behind and twenty miles ahead I couldn't turn if I
wanted to uh oh wrong response don't give me no lip
boy don't reach for that gun boy but officer I don't have
a gun I'm just happy to see you double uh oh some
people have no sense of humor shots are fired your
brains splatter a 9mm is discretely placed in your hand
then those five magic words taught in cop 101 "I feared
for my life," no video no witness no crime ain't nothin'
but a thing.

We think we're slaves? Some slavery is worse than
others. We think our servitude is bad think twice unless
you're Black.

The myth. The great myth. The myth that slavery
ended when Bobby Lee took the quill from Ulysses
Grant and signed on the dotted line the great war is over
slavery is abolished emancipation is proclaimed free at
last free at last well don't be too fast loosening your
shackles. Good old Abe as naïve as he was appealing to

the better angels of our nature why it was all a nasty
disagreement and we did keep it within the family we
forgive you oh sons and daughters of the Noble
Confederacy why we just didn't see eye to eye on a few
things let's let bygones be bygones but the Confederacy
as treacherous as a coiled snake on a flag kept their
hatred alive inside their hearts inside their bones oh
Abraham you should have listened to the whispers of
the darker angels and broken the backs of the traitor
states annexation absorption by the victors the righteous
victors the North was voracious enough to swallow the
South but they were left intact and slavery lived on
manifested in different guise in Jim Crow laws chain
gangs lynchings segregation now segregation tomorrow
segregation forever slavery dies a slow death and
without a stake driven through its heart it will rise again
not that it ever truly fell.

I need to go elsewhere. So much negativity. So
much strife hatred and brutality. What's the matter with
you people anyway? A flawed but decent man once
asked, "Can't we just get along?" A simple and
innocent question a bit odd perhaps in light of his
having been beaten half to death by a phalanx of White
racist cops getting their ya yas by subjugating a big
Black buck. And the city of Los Angeles the city of the
angels nearly burned to the ground when his
oppressors, their brutality rendered forever on video,
were acquitted. It ain't nothin' but a thing.

Was Sisyphus in fact a Black slave, rolling the great bolder of freedom up the steep mountain and just when he thought the backbreaking soul breaking ordeal was finished, when he thought he was free at last free at last, the boulder slipping from his grasp just before the summit, rolling back to the bottom so near and yet so far so much struggle so much turmoil endured then having to start all over again. Regression is the equal and opposite reaction to progression maybe Newton called it right so to all of you slaves remember your roots and loosened shackles can be ratcheted back up at the drop of a hat so watch each other's backs and when the wind blows keep a tight grip on that snazzy new Stetson.

Evidently you're not infallible. I asked to be taken elsewhere somewhere where there is good and goodness. Try again Red Wings. I know you can do it.

Jean. There was a lady named Jean. How long ago was this? Time and memory always mingle in the mist, the opaque fog shrouding the past. It wasn't very long ago at all, or so it would seem, and yet in my memory I am a child walking through the dense trees to Jean's house.

I am a volunteer. I deliver meals to homebound seniors. I bring meals to Jean. She is special. I never knew my grandparents and Jean is how I imagined the perfect grandma to be- warm, kind and unconditionally loving. I would rap on her door and she would answer thanking me profusely for the delivered food she radiated something bright and warm as the sun, something pure and primal that illuminated her home- should I call it love? Jean was in her late eighties and had suffered a stroke, her vision limited as well by macular degeneration. She sometimes talked nonsense, but I always understood her. "Was it good?" she would ask then she would hug and kiss me, grateful for my presence. I wonder if she knew I was a grown man or through cloud of vision and mind assumed I was a child? Such love from that woman such effusive unconditional love telling me on some days she was so glad I had come home. There were times I felt I truly was coming home oh how I looked forward to seeing you coming home to grandma with a gift a gift of food I cried when you left us Jean I think about you all the time. Whenever I left after delivering your food I walked with a different gait and saw with the clarity taken away from your vision. You, Jean, without even trying, made me a better man.

Alright Red Wings give me cause to wax dark and gloomy as it seems to be a more natural fit for the likes of me. How much of life is perspective and attitude? How do these happy-go-lucky people do it are they all deluded do they live in an alternate universe a zippity-

do-da-zippity-a my oh my what a wonderful day
universe where Mr. Bluebird's on their shoulder where
if life presents lemons then make lemonade (another
insipid old saying that's always annoyed me but as you
might expect not to the degree as "You get my goat"
which remains the champion of annoying sayings). Is
this notion of looking at the bright side and the glass is
half full truly positive and wholesome? How many
people have been shot on the battle field because they
were convinced the bullet was meant for the other guy
how many people have gone to the poor house because
the big jackpot at the casino is just one optimistic roll of
the dice away?

Should I? At some point should I form a
conclusion as to what it's all about? Or conclude it's
not about anything sheer meaninglessness blind
randomness we're just a side effect of an endless
infinite series of mindless causes and absurd effects?
Spill Red Wings- give me a clue a nudge in the right
direction.

I'm tired. I'm tired my dear old friends. Tired of
everything. Of pain of heart break of betrayal of
loneliness. I'm tired of memories and of life. I want to
sleep. It may be time old friends for me to fall asleep
and stop waking up.

Wait. Am I dreaming? Something seems amiss. Something is keeping me awake. Something is penetrating my insularity; not a memory or an idea or a fantasy. But something from outside. A sound. Do I hear a sound, not from within my head but outside? I've been enclosed so long, what <u>is outside?</u> What does it even mean anymore?

An odor. A burnt odor. It's smoke. I'm sure of it. Something is burning outside. But I've been inward and isolated so long I'm no longer sure where outside is or how to get there. This couch has been my world for so long I've forgotten about the outside world in the here and now. For so long I've only known the interior world of my mind.

I shudder. I smell the burning again, more insistent and real. I hear the sound again, now louder and more urgent. It's a horrible pitiful sound. It's the sound of a screaming child.

I can't. I can't just lay here passive and inert. A child is screaming and crying outside. How many times did I scream and cry as a child? I must do something. I, of all people, must do something.

I look. I look at them. Help me Red Wings. Help me move. I know I can do it if you help me. Atonement. I think of atonement. Atonement for passivity in the face of cruelty and injustice. Atonement for Carol. And for a strong frightened little Black girl surrounded by bigots and bullies.

You've moved! You've changed your position. Keep going Red Wings. Inspire me. If you can move then I can move.

We do it! Unsteady at first, but we do it. I'm on my feet, running outside carried by you my friends, my Red Wing friends. I see it. A house on fire. The child, the screaming crying child is trapped inside the house. She screams and my lungs burn. She cries and my eyes fill with her tears. Let's move. Carry me fast Red Wings.

The night is cold. I had forgotten about the night and the cold. It's been so long I've been so long in languid inanimation. Where is everyone? Neighbors, firemen, paramedics? Can it be they haven't been notified? No time to think. No time for conjecture. Go. Through the front door.

Her wails are horrific. Pitiful. Fire is everywhere. Flames and smoke marauding through the house. Up the stairs. They know exactly where to take me. Into her room. Where are her parents? Dead, or perhaps she was left, abandoned, a lost cause, like a sick boy in a hospital charity ward. There! In a corner shuddering in a fetal position. Now or never. I grab her and lift her over my head above the flames. Move Red Wings-faster. You've seen it all, you should know what you're doing. Help me. Carry us out of this hell away from death and out into the cold night. The cold world. Sirens. They've finally arrived. They take the child. Is it possible? She looks frightened but unhurt. We did it my friends. You've never faltered or failed me. Then. Then I'm falling. Then the agony sets in.

I'm burned. My legs and lower body are burned. The paramedics place me on a gurney and I'm lifted into an ambulance. "Take care of the child!" I scream. An I.V. is inserted. So familiar. A jar suspended above, fluid running through a tube. I feel like a frightened child being given a blood transfusion. My clothes below my waist are peeled off. My legs, blood red, wet and blistery. But my feet escaped the fire and they leave my shoes on. Do they know? Could they possibly know? I look at you. Unscathed- unchanged.

Sirens blare. We're moving fast to the E.R. How bad is it? Will I survive?

Through a thickening fog of delirium my thoughts and questions the same ones from a lifetime are returning and finally conclusions are being drawn.

Life. Is it as it so often seems, a protracted nightmare punctuated by an occasional dream? The world is a horrible place. Far more for some than for others. And if it appears meaningless it's because we are too timid to inject meaning into it. If it is uncaring then we must care. I'm strapped to this gurney staring at you my Red Wing Friends. And if I become unconscious and don't wake up you will be my final vision.

And if I awaken, burnt, beaten, but unbroken, you will be my first vision. And if we pull out of this I have an idea.

Yes. The world is a horrible place. Let's give the couch a rest and hit the street. There may be other children in burning houses abandoned and ignored. Let's meet the horrible world head on and give it a run for its money.

And why not? You indomitable Red Wings last forever.

And you <u>do</u> come with a lifetime supply of laces.

About the Author

Ron Terranova is a Huntington Beach, Ca. writer of novels, short stories, poetry and edgy, provocative posts which appear regularly on his blog, rterranova.com. A Pushcart nominee, his poetry has appeared most recently in *Chiron Review*. He is the author of *October Light* and its sequel, *October Twilight*, both collections of dark short fiction, and the novel *I, Polyphemus*. He began writing at age eleven, after nearly dying from a serious illness. He is a strong believer that art in all its forms can hasten and facilitate the healing process.

More by Ron Terranova

October Twilight: A Book Of Short Fiction

I, Polyphemus

More by REaDLips Press:

How to Throw a Psychic a Surprise Party – Noreen Lace

Tourists in the Country of Love – Jo Rousseau

Baby Doll – Nicolette Elzie

UPCOMING RELEASES

Halfway to Impossible – M.R. Koch

Our Gentle Sins – Noreen Lace 21/22

Ron Terranova

Made in the USA
Columbia, SC
24 November 2021

49679579R00109